EXPORT AGENTS

A Complete Guide to their
Selection and Control

THE WORLD AS 14 MARKET SUPERVISION AREAS

Each area can be delegated to a resident Factory Representative who supervises the agents in each country or region

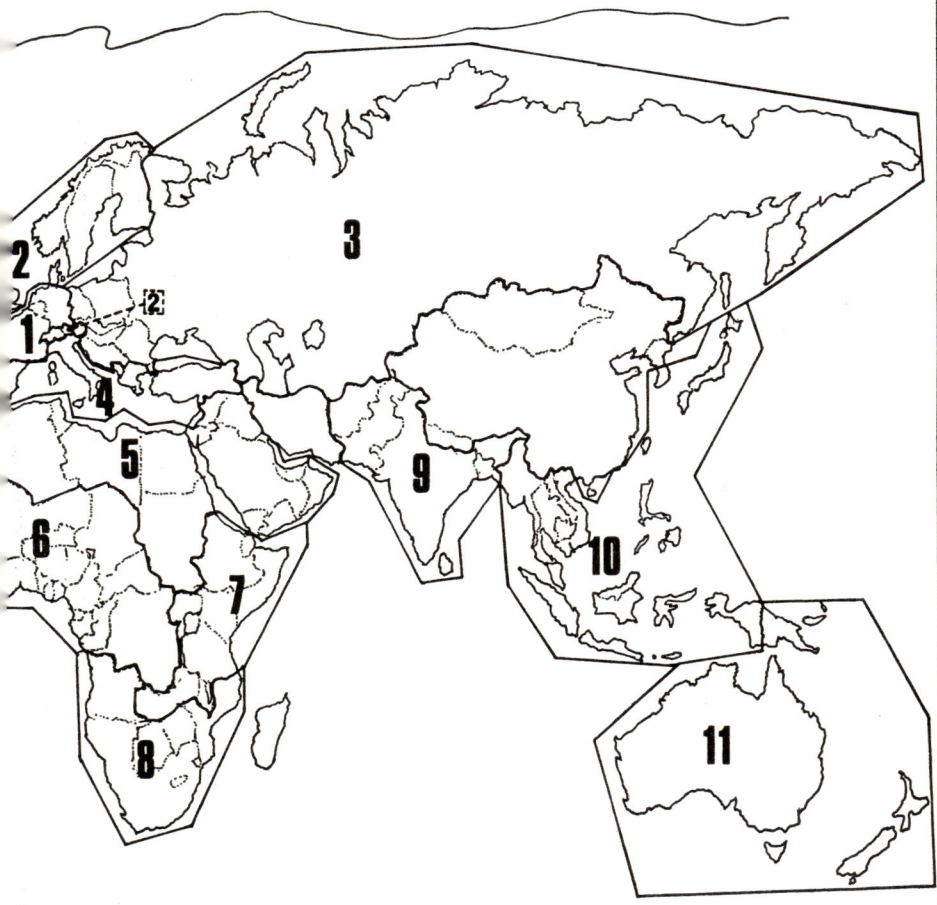

7. East Africa
Kenya, Tanzania, Uganda, Zambia, Malawi, Ethiopia, Somalia

8. Southern and Central Africa
Republic of South Africa, Rhodesia, Angola, Mozambique

9. Indian sub-continent
India, Pakistan, Ceylon

10. South-East Asia
Burma, Thailand, Laos, Cambodia, Vietnam, Malaysia, Singapore, Indonesia, Philippines, Taiwan, Hong Kong, Japan

11. Australia, New Zealand

12. Canada, USA

13. Central America and Caribbean
(including) Mexico, Guatemala, Belise (British Honduras), Nicaragua, Costa Rica, Panama, Bahamas, Jamaica, Trinidad

14. South America
Guiana, Venezuela, Colombia, Ecuador, Peru, Bolivia, Brazil, Paraguay, Uruguay, Chile, Argentina

China and neighbours are not included in a market area. Other territories can be left to individual circumstances, e.g. Iran or Malagasy Republic (Madagascar)

EXPORT AGENTS

A Complete Guide to their Selection and Control

COLIN McMILLAN
and
SYDNEY PAULDEN

Gower Press

First Published in Great Britain by Gower Press Limited
140 Great Portland Street, London W1N 5TA
1968
Second impression 1969

Set in 11 on 12 point Imprint
Printed in Great Britain by
The Camelot Press Ltd
London and Southampton

Contents

The Authors

COLIN McMILLAN has travelled widely to almost every country in the world during service in the Royal Navy and in industry. He has visited the USSR frequently in selling on behalf of ICI, and subsequently travelled throughout Western Europe as Managing Director of Management Selection Group's subsidiary specialising in agent and distributor selection. He was director of the East European Department of the Overseas Marketing Corporation, where he was responsible for the sales of British products to the countries of the COMECON bloc.

SYDNEY PAULDEN is acknowledged as a specialist writer on international trade. For eight years he was Editorial Director of Envoy Journals Limited, publishers of the journals *Industrial Intelligence* and *Industrial Envoy*. He has made industrial tours of a variety of countries, including Japan, Finland, Israel, Germany, and Czechoslovakia. These tours enabled him to meet and interview factory managers, export directors, ministers of foreign trade, import agents, and buyers in many industries.

Mr Paulden holds an MA degree from Cambridge. His foreign languages include French, German, Italian and some Finnish, Swedish and Spanish. He is the author of *Plan Your Export Drive* which was published in 1965. The book is used widely in the UK as a textbook for marketing and export management courses; it is also in use throughout the world on courses to train commercial attachés. In 1969 Mr Paulden was awarded a Winston Churchill Fellowship on marketing.

Acknowledgements

The experience of many hundreds of exporters, agents and official organisations has been distilled in this book. However, the following have been especially helpful in providing material and the authors would like to offer them their gratitude:

Associated Industrial Consultants Ltd
Australia and New Zealand Bank Ltd
Bank of London and South America
Barclays Bank DCO
Board of Trade, Export Services Branch
British Agents Register
British Export Houses Association
British National Committee, International Chamber of Commerce
British National Export Council
Chase Manhattan Bank
Dean, Warburg Ltd
First National City Bank
Hungarian Chamber of Commerce
Industrial Market Research Ltd
Institute of Export
International Chamber of Commerce, Paris
Int. Union of Commercial Agents and Brokers, Amsterdam
Japan External Trade Organisation
London Chamber of Commerce
Manufacturers Agents Association of Great Britain and Ireland Inc
MSL Export Services Ltd
PA Management Consultants Ltd
Polish Chamber of Foreign Trade
United Africa Group
United Nations Statistical Department
Waterlow and Sons Ltd
Westminster Bank Limited
Yugoslav Federal Chamber of Economy

CHAPTER 1

Seven True Stories About
Export Agents

The characters in the following fables are not fictitious. They bear
a resemblance to many living exporters.

1 ——————————————————————————————

A manufacturer had an inquiry from Germany for his range of
electrical components. After due negotiation the inquiry was
converted into good business. The German customer assembled
switchboards and required a continuous supply of these components. In turn, he sold his switchboards to other German
industries. The exporter and the switchboard manufacturer
prospered.

Eventually this favoured German customer suggested to the
exporter that the range of electrical components could be sold to
other customers in Germany and that he would be willing to take
on the sole agency for the market. The exporter agreed, partly
from his eagerness to fall in with the wishes of his client and partly
from idleness.

But after such a fruitful start, the progress charts for that
market refused to swell. They remained barren.

The exporter called in an outside adviser and the German
market was thoroughly examined. The findings were announced.
The major potential for the exporter of those particular electrical
components was to factories assembling switchboards. The agent
himself was one of these and found it very awkward to sell his
principal's components to his own immediate competitors.

The exporter was obliged to cancel the agency agreement with his former best customer. In his place he appointed another German firm which produced a complementary range of components and which had access without obstacle to all potential clients. This new arrangement worked very effectively, except that the former agent was no longer such a big purchaser of the components.

Moral. Don't spoil a beautiful courtship with marriage.

2

In one ex-colonial territory there was a steady, moderate sale of a certain commodity of very high quality, packed in decorative tins. It cost about 50 cents a tin. Sales were handled through a local agent, with the importing done by a merchant who was the main customer.

The merchant suddenly saw his retail business in this line threatened by a new competitor importing a slightly cheaper product. He approached the local agent but the latter was reluctant to make any special efforts to beat this competition. Turnover was too small to justify it.

The merchant, however, made a direct approach to the manufacturer in a distant land, pointing out that the line would shortly have to be discontinued if nothing was done.

The manufacturer was prompted to send out one of their own marketing experts to investigate the market from scratch. They discovered some surprising things.

The sales of that particular pack were entirely a leftover from the colonial days. The white planters had shipped in the very expensive high-quality product they could afford. Their servants had also become accustomed to using it and had gone on purchasing small quantities after independence.

It was obvious after a minimum of research that the existing pack was far too highly priced ever to become generally acceptable. Moreover, the product had never been matched to the market in any scientific way. It had just filtered in haphazardly. It had to be mixed with water and this, because of the high local chlorine content, produced poor colour and inferior taste.

A proper market survey was carried out. It was found that if the commodity's price and taste were changed there was a potential market at least twenty times more valuable than the one being reached with the unsuitable pack.

A new blend was produced which not only mixed well with the chlorine but was also far cheaper to make and sell.

The costly decorated tin was dispensed with and instead 1-cent packs were brought on to the market. The product immediately became available to everybody in a 50-million population instead of to a few with strangely acquired tastes.

Sales grew so rapidly that in a short time the manufacturer and the merchant set up a joint venture factory on the spot to cater for local demands. The competitor who had originally started the scare sold out to the new partnership.

Chewing over the facts later, the exporter realised that he had been satisfied with an annual turnover from the territory of about £60 000 ($150 000) which gave him absolutely no trouble. He had never visited the market to find out what happened to those pretty tins he was shipping out there. The local agent, for his part, was making about 5 per cent which provided £3000 ($7500) towards overheads. This was roughly equivalent to the cost of maintaining half of one salesman per annum, when salary, office space, travel expenses and commission are considered. Without an injection of cash and enthusiasm from the exporter, there would be little likelihood of an agent risking his own time and money on expanding the market. The agent had never been educated about his principal's product and had no idea even that there could be different blends to suit different conditions or a choice of packs to suit a variety of pockets.

Moral. Underpaid servants are expensive.

3 ────────────────────────────────────

Once when a new export director took over a big company's international sales he was rather horrified at the firm's poor performance in Europe. Every market was sluggish.

One of his first actions was to call in an outside consultant and commission a thorough investigation of the efficiency of every agent they had in Europe.

The consultant went to work. He surveyed the potential in each country for his client's product and then personally interviewed the agent there. He questioned him on his share of the market, on his growth compared with competitors, on the rate of increase in sales, on the productivity of each of the agent's salesmen. The consultant made it quite clear what he was doing. He was preparing a report for the export director which would enable him to rethink his whole agency structure in Europe and make changes where these were obviously necessary.

These researches took about six months. At the end of this time the consultant came back to the export director with a big dossier and a sheaf of recommendations.

"I think these are no longer necessary," said the export director, "but thank you, just the same. In the period during your investigations all our agents have increased their sales by 200 per cent!"

Moral. Water boils best when there's a fire underneath it.

4

A group of companies on the mainland of Europe had interests in many fields. It had what it liked to term "a network of international agents." One day the sales manager of one member company approached group head office because he wanted to launch his particular products on the British market where he had no previous experience. Group head office looked through its card index and put him in touch with its London agent. Plans were made to launch the new products at an exhibition.

Unfortunately it turned out that the only group products previously marketed in Britain through that agent were garden furniture and household rubber-ware. The sales manager wanted to introduce highly specialised chemical plant, but he was obliged to employ his group's "network."

In all fairness, it has to be said that the London agent did his very best, but he was just not familiar with the field. Some orders were obtained, but on all matters relating to applications, specifications, maintenance, and even specialised packing, he was out of his depth.

As a result the unfortunate sales manager was constantly

involved in additional expense, being obliged to send his engineers over to London far more frequently than necessary to straighten out fairly simple problems. And, of course, nothing like the market potential was achieved. The agent was intelligent enough to appreciate this, but he was not too happy at the thought of introducing an alternative agent to serve his big group masters. The sales manager was caught in an international network which merely hindered his efforts.

Moral. A web may suit the spider but not the fly.

5 ——————————————————————————

Somehow or other the managing director of an English firm once looked at some export statistics. He was amazed to see that large quantities of his particular line were being sold to Italy.

"Jim," he said to his sales director, "go to Italy and appoint agents, soon as you can."

Jim was not too keen on this idea. He did not quite know where to start. He made some inquiries and commissioned some market research. Whilst this was being prepared he stayed out of the managing director's way so he couldn't ask him why he was not in Italy.

The market research results came up very quickly, with a very definite recommendation. "Don't appoint agents. Do a direct selling job yourself."

It had been discovered that for their line there was a small number of very easily identifiable buyers. They were all situated in a compact area easily reached from Milan. They had a pattern of buying every two or three months at specific times according to a seasonal cycle. Furthermore, these buyers were particularly inclined towards dealing direct with the manufacturer, because they liked to have an influence on designs for the following seasons.

The sales director did a direct selling job very successfully. The managing director still hankered after agents but was finally convinced by the first year's results.

Moral. Bosses are often wrong, but sometimes they have to be told.

6

A chocolate beverage manufacturer had command of many markets throughout the world. His problem usually was one of increasing production sufficiently to meet all his orders. His experts came up with a method of streamlining production which involved producing a granular product instead of one in powder form. This was launched with success on the home market after a big advertising and re-education campaign.

However, soon after its introduction to the export markets, the agent in a big market sent an urgent report that the product was going hard in the tin. The manufacturer ignored this, possibly believing it was a panic move merely because the new product was a little unfamiliar. He thought that in foreign places the consumer might be puzzled by the difference between a powder and granules.

But the complaints continued to stream in from the agent by cable.

Finally, after great delay, samples showed that the agent was in fact right. The product *was* going hard in the container. The trouble was not with the product. It was with the container. The cans had an inefficient seam which was not air tight. The long journey to warm, wet climates meant that the granules caked together, a phenomenon which did not take place in the early days of launching on the home market, where weather conditions were more favourable and stocks were being cleared very rapidly.

By the time the can-sealing machine had been overhauled, there were large numbers of dissatisfied customers and irate agents overseas. In one territory the market share dropped from 90 to 50 per cent.

Moral. The agent may be foreign, but he is occasionally right.

7

One firm had been doing direct selling in an important market because it had not been able to locate an agent with a good enough sales approach. Then suddenly it found a new man who was setting up as an agent and had an outstanding sales record in a related field.

They brought him back to head office, signed him up and gave him exclusive rights to a large territory with an attractive rate of commission. He asked for and got a very long-term contract.

Being an excellent salesman, he sold himself well to a number of principals and soon had an impressive string of accounts. This meant expanding his business and hiring new staff. He took on salesmen. Because of the extreme shortage of good salesmen he had to take on people of inferior quality—far below his own standard. His own time was taken up with running his business administration from behind his desk.

Within a very short time the exporting firm found itself represented in this lucrative market by the poor salesmen it had itself previously refused to employ. It had failed to specify in the agreement that the agent himself was to do the selling on their behalf. Their agreement was with the company he had set up; and it tied up their market for a long time.

Moral. It is foolish to look the horse in the mouth and then take home the ass.

THE LESSONS TO BE LEARNT

Any manufacturer who cannot see some reflection of his own experience in those stories is a man in a million and his case history should be written up as a guide to others, for a large number of different research surveys have shown that the selection and control of export agents is a disastrously neglected aspect of international business.

It is estimated that over half of the world's foreign trade is handled by agents. According to the United Nations' Statistical Department, world-wide imports in 1967 totalled 202 000 million US dollars. This would mean that agents placed orders for more than $100 000 million worth of goods. American exporters would have paid commission on about $15 000 million to agents in foreign markets. British exporters would have handed out commission on at least £2000 million sterling.

This is big money in any language or currency and yet research proves how lackadaisical is the approach of the majority of business-men in seeing they are getting real value for money. One survey by a London firm of consultants investigated the techniques of fifty-one export directors, each employing between forty and fifty overseas agents. As many as 42 per cent admitted they did not check their agents' promotional methods before appointing them. A mere 2 per cent of these experts had visited more than half of their agents in the previous year, whilst 14 per cent had visited none at all.

Believe it or not, but 12 per cent normally spent nothing at all for the purpose of selecting and appointing their agents, 54 per cent laid out less than £200 a time and only 6 per cent consciously invested more. The remainder were not at all sure what money was involved.

It is hardly surprising to note, therefore, that the 2000 or more agents employed by the respondents produced fairly meagre turnover figures on average. Less than £10 000 a year per agent was confessed by 12 per cent, less than £20 000 by 6 per cent and under £50 000 by 8 per cent. Only one-tenth of the exporters could claim that their agents were averaging more than £50 000 turnover. It was probably to be expected, unfortunately, that the great majority of the manufacturers interviewed had no means of answering this particular question.

In a comparative study between home market and export market selling methods, it was found that the area sales supervisors at home had to report personally to the sales manager about once a week, whereas the equivalent overseas agent was seen not more than once a year. Among smaller organisations, the home sales manager will call on his local salesmen roughly thirty times a year, whilst the export manager gets round to his overseas staff about once in every three years.

In a review of firms and their exports, PEP (Political and Economic Planning) carried out a questionnaire survey financed by the Nuffield Foundation. Out of 471 firms, 174 had increased their exports during the previous five-year period. Two-thirds of these owed their success to new sales efforts, whilst only 19 per cent attributed it to improved production and only 15 per cent to any change of demand or competition or terms of trade. The major types of new sales efforts were increased promotion, entering of new markets, change of overseas agents, stepping up of visits to

8

agents, increased stocking with agents, and supervision of increased local promotion by agents.

The facts indicate that it is worth the while of all exporters to investigate the productivity of their foreign representation and to approach the selection and control of their agents in a thorough and scientific manner. Many exporters treat the agent as something of a difficult toad. A touch of a not-too-magic wand could transform him into a fairy prince.

CHAPTER 2

Pinpointing the Agent by Defining the Market

After interviewing officials from banks, government offices, and trading companies, considerable sympathy is felt for those people whose job it is to help to find agents for would-be exporters.

It is incredible how much time and effort is wasted by ignorance. Mountains of frustration are created because of a lack of knowledge about markets and type of agent required, and because of a lack of preparation to service an agent if he is appointed.

RESEARCH

There are two main reasons for researching export markets. These are: (*a*) maximum profitability, and (*b*) maximum exploitation.

It is the exporter's responsibility to select his key markets. The world is a big place and no company can afford to launch into the whole of it at one go. Everyone is working from limited resources and these must be applied in the most productive manner possible.

When the key markets have been isolated, then each must be researched in depth. Simultaneously, the exporter's own company must be analysed to discover the major factors which influence profitability through exports.

When this has been achieved, the exporter will be able to produce a detailed pen picture of the type of agent he requires in the exact market he wishes to cover. It is at that point that the search can begin for the likely candidate overseas. This approach will bring many benefits:

1   It will prevent waste of effort in appointing agents in unprofitable territories
2   It will greatly increase the likelihood of locating the most suitable agent in the best markets
3   It will provide basic knowledge of the market and its future potential which will help to guide and control the agent effectively
4   It will impress and therefore stimulate all the people involved in helping the exporter to develop the market

It is hardly possible to exaggerate the dampening effect that a half-hearted approach has on executives who are expected to help to locate an agent. One banker told of a businessman coming on to his stand at an exhibition and asking: "Where can I export to? I make parachutes." Another visited an organisation specialising in Latin America and had never even studied a map of the area. He was surprised to learn he might have to appoint an agent in each country there, a lengthy and possibly costly business if you have no order of priorities.

SELF-ANALYSIS

There is no government which is not currently urging its businessmen to export more to earn foreign currency. To a government, there is a big difference between foreign sales and transactions on the home market. It regards business conducted between firms at home almost as "interdepartmental." A country really only earns money through exports.

But this is not the way that the individual firms look at exports. To them all sales are sales and are judged on the merits of their profitability. This is why so much government exhortation is ineffective. On the other hand too many manufacturers shy away from exports as a result of a misconception. They automatically imagine that transport costs and agents' commissions will either slash profitability or price their products out of the market.

The opposite is often the true picture. Exports can very frequently help a company to maximise returns on its investment. When a certain share has been established of a home market, any increase can demand a disproportionate amount of promotional effort, whereas very rapid increase in sales can be the initial result of penetrating a completely new market overseas. If there is spare production capacity in the factory, then the increased sales will add very little to fixed overheads. Their cost will merely comprise materials consumed, some extra labour and actual transport and distribution.

Costed in this way, it often turns out that the extra production for export earns a high profit in proportion to the extra investment.

If these factors are analysed with precision, then it is actually possible to determine what size of market should be developed overseas to maximise returns before additional plant and capital investment are required. It also makes it possible to define exactly the real minimum limits when deciding a pricing policy to compete in foreign markets.

Similarly, this knowledge of your own production profile makes it possible to determine at what point in future expansion it is necessary to add a fixed overhead factor to export costing. Self-knowledge gives strength and resolution to the approach to new markets and helps considerably to assess the wisdom of further investment in overseas promotion, the advisability of establishing a branch office or factory to serve a foreign market, or to judge correctly the moment to set up further agents in new territories.

KEY MARKETS

With so many markets in the world to choose from, why choose the wrong ones? Ask a hundred exporters which markets they sell to and why, and the majority will tell you that they happened to receive orders or inquiries through their name "percolating" overseas; or they were approached by an agent who thought he could do something for them in his area; or they decided to join in a specialist exhibition which their trade association or trade ministry happened to be mounting in some country or other.

This really explains why so many agents are so sadly neglected. They are treated almost like "squatters," people who happen to be settled on a territory through no specific intention of the principal. No move is made to clear them off, but on the other hand nothing is done to see that they are comfortable and productively employed.

A very small minority of firms is in a position to market effectively in a large number of foreign territories. It is essential for most to husband their resources and concentrate exclusively on key markets picked for their high profitability potential. Sometimes it might be better for a government to set up a council to prevent firms from exporting. As it is at present, there is a multiplicity of official organisations pushing different markets and fighting for converts amongst the uninitiated manufacturers like canvassers before an election. For an election this is in order, for once the votes are cast little attention is paid to the movements of the converts until the next election comes round. But this is not so with exporting. Casting the vote for a market is the very first step. After that comes a three- or four-year period of launch and consolidation which must be done with the wholehearted support of representation on the spot. There is little chance of consolidation when a firm has been drummed into going on a mission to Japan, the Philippines, Hong Kong, Thailand, and India, into exhibiting in Czechoslovakia, appointing an agent in Brazil and attending a conference on Scandinavia.

Key markets must be explored from many aspects. For example:

1   Is there any embargo on the export of your products from your home country to the market?
2   Is there any restriction on their importation there?
3   Are your potential customers permitted to transfer payment from their country to yours?
4   What is the total market value in your line?
5   What is the share you could achieve?
6   Who are the potential buyers?
7   What price would be competitive?
8   What is the strength of the competition?
9   Is business obtained by hidden discounts to special major outlets?
10   What design or packaging features are involved?
11   Which are the most important features which influence buying decisions?
12   What is the geographical concentration of the major sales outlets?
13   What is the trend of sales?
14   What forms of distribution are necessary and available?

15   What technique of selling is called for?
16   What credit terms are normal?

The answers to questions like these, coupled with any special considerations of your own product (maintenance, spares, stocks, instruction, etc), will enable the exporter to draw up a very precise agency profile; alternatively, they might indicate that a licensee is preferable or that a joint venture with a local firm is called for.

If the obvious approach is via a commission agent, then the exporter can make use of the many services available to help in locating an agent to the best effect. Trade attachés at embassies, managers of local banks, information officers at trade associations, liaison officers at agency federations—all will be aided and encouraged in locating firms or individuals who match up as nearly as possible to the portrait of the perfect agent for the product to be introduced.

Furthermore, a much more intelligent agreement can be drawn up with the selected agent on the basis of what the exporter knows about the value and potential of the market. Realistic targets can be set. Requests from the agent for promotional support can be met or refused according to the detailed knowledge gained of how the market works. Although it is a good thing to select an agent whose judgement you can trust, it is not advisable to be solely dependent upon his judgement. Only when the exporter is properly prepared with some market expertise of his own can he distinguish between well-clothed ideas and pure flannel.

It must also be remembered that in many instances you have to fight hard to get the agent to select you. It is easy to find an agent, but very difficult to find a good one. When you have found a good one you have to convince him that he will find a relationship with you especially profitable. He exists to make his own business as profitable as possible. He will prefer a well-organised, marketing-orientated principal. The exporter who knows what he is doing and why he is doing it will be most likely to attract an agent to match. If an agent is content to bumble along with a vague principal then he is not likely to produce any dynamic results. Similarly, an efficient, energetic agent will not tolerate the frustration and loss of business stemming from a sluggish partner. You can usually spot a good agent from the companies he keeps.

PROFILE OF AGENT AND PRINCIPAL

The kind of details of your company and product which ought to be given when looking for an agent will vary considerably from case to case. Similarly, the pen-portrait which can be drawn of the ideal agent will depend upon product, territory, stage of development, and type of selling needed.

Accordingly, it is always extremely difficult to lay down any rules or offer any specific pattern to be followed. However, it is still surprising how scanty the information often is which is requested by organisations which offer help in this field. Many proforma exist which require such a tiny amount of information to complete them that one wonders how this can really help to narrow the field when picking out likely agency candidates. In the same way, many so-called agency registers offer such a paucity of data about the firms or individuals on the roll that the principal can waste a considerable amount of time checking with candidates who are quite unsuitable.

When setting out to locate the right representation, the best method is to be as detailed as possible, then if no one can be found to suit the exact description it might be necessary to settle for the nearest. At least, in that way, everyone knows what he is looking for, what factors are important and which candidates would be a waste of time from the start. Too frequently the search for an agent, especially when it is done as a free service by an official or semi-official organisation, turns out to be a hunt for any agent willing to take on the product, rather than the scrupulous location of an agent who can really penetrate the market to the maximum.

Having said this, it might be of some value to present checklists of possible data which can be compiled before the final search begins:

1   The Principal and his Products
(*a*)   Type of company: public, private, partnership, one-man; capital rating; turnover; directors
(*b*)   Brief history
(*c*)   Outline of future plans; new lines; expansion
(*d*)   Number of people employed; number and size of factories and branch offices

(e)   Range of products
(f)   Size and share of home market

2   Export Brief
(a)   Country or countries where agent required
(b)   Nature of product or products to be handled
(c)   Price range
(d)   Applications
(e)   Units of measurement
(f)   How packaged
(g)   Manufacturing capacity situation
(h)   Existing export markets
(i)   Rate of expansion in exports

3   Price and Payment Consideration
(a)   Quotations in f.o.b., c.i.f., c.i.f. duty paid, or other terms
(b)   Currency of quotations
(c)   Import duty rate / Brussels Nomenclature
(d)   Turnover tax / TVA / other form of transmission tax
(e)   Who determines price to ultimate customer?
(f)   Commission range offered
(g)   Terms of payment
(h)   Who invoices?
(i)   Discounts for quantity or prompt payment

4   Market Brief
(a)   Is extra market research required?
(b)   Is the principal willing to meet costs?
(c)   Has research been done on suitability of product for the market?
(d)   Main competitors in market
(e)   Who represents them?
(f)   What are sales advantages over competition?

5   Sales Promotion
(a)   Recommended methods of selling and promotion
(b)   Who is to be responsible for promotion?
(c)   What target rates are specified?
(d)   Sales literature arrangements

(e)   Agent briefing and training facilities

6   Agency Definition
(a)   Recommended size—big, small, individual
(b)   Capital backing required and why
(c)   Desirable co-products
(d)   Forbidden competitive product range
(e)   Entrée to which type of outlets?
(f)   Specialist type of salesmen or technicians
(g)   Essential location of sales offices
(h)   Number and location of service depots
(i)   Warehouse and stockist facilities required
(j)   Desirable transport facilities

The profiles which are eventually produced will to a certain extent be simple answers to these questions, whilst any very important points will be enlarged upon for the benefit of the prospective agent. For example, a full description ought to be given of the type of outlets to which the agent should have an entrée, for usually this experience is the agent's greatest value to the principal. This is the expertise which would cost the principal a large amount of money and effort to acquire in a new market. It is surprising to see how often this aspect of an agent's work is inadequately checked before he is appointed, with the result that he has to introduce himself to a completely new range of customers for the new product. Consequently there is a long and painful delay before the market is opened up.

Any of the points listed above can give a lead to someone along the line. If the inquiry is being handled via the commercial counsellor at an embassy, he might well be aware of the competitive product mentioned and latch on to an agent he knows is able to compete.

If a large amount of capital backing is needed to launch the product successfully, then the branch manager of a bank will not bother to send back names of people or firms he knows could not meet this requirement.

Similarly, with the information available about the principal, prospective agents can withdraw at an early stage if the product and the manufacturer do not fit in with their own plans for development.

The opposite is also true. If the detailed profile appears to fit a candidate very closely, or if the description of the product and the principal are just what an agent is looking for, then the whole process can be speeded up. The people involved will be encouraged to take positive steps. The matter will become more real in their eyes, not merely a paper inquiry. In all business matters there is a need to compete: to compete against the other manufacturers demanding time for their inquiries; to compete against those other items which are calling for the agent's attention; to compete against the other bits of paper somebody has to read and take action on.

If the principal can show by his preparation and his methods that he is determined, knowledgeable, shrewd, thorough and accurate, from afar, with the material he presents, then he will gain enormous benefits. Claiming personal attention is a very big step in the right direction.

The well-documented application for help in finding an agent would shine out amongst the general run of ill-prepared inquiries. These usually consist of nothing more than the name of the manufacturer, a brief remark that he has a high reputation at home, and a handful of leaflets describing the product to be exported. It is the sort of application which inspires no one and which is liable to produce a list of unsuitable potential agents.

It will be explained later (see Chapter 4) that most inquiry channels are long chains of officials who are not specialised in the product being handled. If the material given into their hands does not speak for itself, then there is no one to speak for it.

18

CHAPTER 3

Twenty-seven Types of Agency

To call a spade a spade can be very confusing. There is a folk museum in Ireland which displays over fifty types of spade used in that country alone. Goodness knows how many different types exist in the whole world. And the point is that each variation is just right for one job and just wrong for another. The one designed to dig out potatoes is no use for cutting peat.

The same is true of "agents."

It should be considered an accident of language that only one vague term, "agent," has become a portmanteau expression for a multitude of different types of representation. The efficient exporter should consider all the permutations and define the type best suited to his product and best marketing approach. This will enable him and his helpers to find or set up exactly the right organisation to develop a foreign market to its fullest potential.

Types of agent can be divided and sub-divided in many ways. In order to appreciate their different functions they might be seen in four major classifications:

I   Agent acting for the exporter who is the principal
II   Agent purchasing for himself as principal
III   Agent acting for other buyers as principals
IV   Agent undertaking specialised aspect of export cycle other than selling: financing, shipping, warehousing, etc

There is no single definitive way of listing the different possibilities, The following are examples of how the type of agent might be analysed. It might help to clarify the exporter's own ideas on his requirements and contribute to a specific definition which will simplify the work of others involved in locating the best organisation.

I: AGENT ACTING FOR EXPORTER AS PRINCIPAL

1 Agent on Commission He can be responsible for the whole, or part, or none of the *del credere* risk. His rate of commission will take into account his financial risk and it might be on a sliding scale to provide the correct system of motivation.

The straightforward commission agent is not a party to the contract made between the customer and the principal. He is simply the selling link, bringing the two parties together in return for his commission.

This arrangement, probably the most common of all, is generally most suitable where long-term selling is required to a fairly large number of possible customers. Turnover in the market is not likely to justify setting up the exporter's own sales operation, so it is convenient to share the agent's time. His overheads are covered by the commission he earns from a number of principals, either foreign exporters or possibly also local manufacturers.

The principal also benefits from the cross-fertilisation of sales contacts which the agent gains by representing several ranges of products, assuming they are carefully chosen to relate to a similar market without being competitive.

2 Commission / Fee and Commission / Stockist Agencies. There are types of agencies set up on a part commission basis. Occasionally it is wise to provide a fee or retainer to permit the agent to earn some revenue when there is a long development period expected before commission can be earned regularly. Without part fee it might be difficult to launch a new product, as the agent could be unwilling to risk too much of his own time and money selling an untried product. The fee can be on a phasing-out basis, with pure commission taking over after a given selling-in period. Even when an agent is working on commission for some products, he might be offered a retainer to introduce a new range from the same principal.

Similarly, if the principal has a number of different lines to be marketed, the agent can work on a commission for some of the products which are slow and he can be expected to purchase stocks for resale of those lines with a quick turnover. Separate agreements have to be made with the agent for each method of operation. Stocks on consignment, to be sold on commission, should remain the property of the exporter until sold. The exporter would normally be responsible for all charges for import and transport to ensure that the goods remained his property and not part of the agent's in the event of bankruptcy or winding-up. All investment in those goods would be the principal's. Any money paid by a customer in advance for those goods in stock would be the principal's, merely held on his account by the agent.

On the other hand, the range of goods bought into stock by the agent would be the agent's property and he would normally be responsible for all charges relating to them. This will depend upon the contract signed with him. The agent sells the goods and makes his own profit on them.

3 Salaried Salesmen. If there is a lot of non-profitable customer contact work involved in selling the product, if the sales story necessitates a considerable amount of training and up-dating, and if it is essential for the salesman to make frequent calls on a very large number of potential clients, then the best means of selling is likely to be through a salaried salesman. A local national, he would become an employee of the principal and the principal would be responsible for the insurance, welfare, holiday pay, and so on of the salesman according to local law. The salesman would be licensed to accept orders on behalf of the principal and his expenses, to an agreed amount, would be met for him.

He could work from home or from an overseas sales office set up by the principal to supervise the selling over a wide area.

It is possible for this kind of salesman or sales office to be shared by exporters with complementary products. They can control the selling directly and agree terms for the cover of overheads and expenses. As he is benefiting from a regular salary (plus commission if incentives are required) he can readily spare the time for training at regular intervals.

4 Independent Salesmen. There exists in some of the more developed countries, such as in the Common Market, a breed of commercial traveller who has his own round of sales calls on retailers or wholesalers or factories. He obtains the right to act on behalf of a number of different principals and can accept orders in their names. He operates from home with very small overheads and works on a commission basis. He is reluctant to become involved in highly specialised selling, for he cannot afford to lose good selling time at training sessions. He covers his own expenses and is technically self-employed for purposes of insurance and other local requirements.

Being a one-man concern, with perhaps the help of his wife, he cannot undertake to stock goods, service them or become involved with the laborious procedures of importation. He merely takes orders and passes them on to the principal, thus qualifying for a commission.

This type of salesman is very suitable if there are comparatively few customers for any one principal, so that it is hardly worth the manufacturer's while to engage a salaried man, and if the goods are relatively simple to understand and sell. It also suits situations where the average orders are small so that again it is hardly worth the manufacturer's while to pay all the expenses involved in visiting the client, although the salesman can earn sufficient commission by obtaining orders for more than one product line.

Another aspect to bear in mind is the availability of the goods to be exported. Some manufacturers have a surplus of goods at one time and a shortage another time. It would be uneconomic to have a salaried salesman lying idle for part of the year. It would also not suit the agency firm which wishes to build up a continuing expanding business. The independent man can add your product to his list when it is available and simply not offer it on his rounds when it is not.

When working with this sort of selling, the exporter may have to appoint ancillary agencies to handle other aspects of the export process, such as warehousing, transportation, and debt collecting, paying for these services as and when they are required.

5 Agent / Distributor. This is the instance where the agent works on commission for, say, the sale of machinery but works on profit for the sale and distribution of consumables or spares related to the product. The exporter is the contracting party with the customer for the machine, but the customer purchases the consumables directly from the agent in his own right. The agent would normally be expected to purchase stocks of the consumables in order to offer the right service to clients who had installed the machinery. The agent may or may not, according to agreement, purchase the supplies from an alternative source (for example, a local printer if it is stationery associated with office machinery).

6 Agent / Warehousing. Some products require the type of marketing best suited to a commission agent but, in addition, call for warehousing facilities. The arrangement can be normal commission for sales with a fee or rental in addition to meet the agent's extra overheads.

7 Agent / Servicing Company. Large items of capital equipment, such as cranes, machine tools and heavy chemical plant, cannot be bought by the agent and must be handled on a commission on sales basis. At the same time, the selling process involves specialist installation, regular maintenance, and a spares and repairs service. It is essential for the exporter's lasting reputation in the market that these aspects are not neglected. A fair arrangement is for the agent to guarantee certain minimum service facilities in return for a direct charge, often related proportionately to the increasing size of the problem as more and more machines are sold.

8 Agent / Design Office. A surprisingly large number of products lean heavily on a design service in the selling approach. This is true of specialised factory flooring, prefabricated buildings, storage shelving and racking, central heating or air conditioning installations, where each sale can only be the result of a survey of the client's problem plus a satisfactory design solution. Experts have to inspect the site and specify the equipment needed.

For this reason a number of exporters need to appoint an agent who can offer drawing office facilities where the specifications are worked out, then agreed by the client and used to order the materials or components from the principal. The agent is paid for these services separately from the commission earned on the orders themselves.

It does not automatically follow that the agent carries out the installations, for these are frequently best completed by local contractors convenient to each client's site, sometimes even organised and paid for by the customer rather than the agent or the principal. There is very big international business being conducted in prefabricated factory buildings which are designed by men on the spot, ordered in bundles of components from the exporting manufacturer, and left to the would-be factory owner to see to the foundation preparation and the erection with his own choice of builder.

9 Agent / Customer. Sometimes there is a major customer in a particular market who is willing to offer the exporter's products to other potential customers on a commission basis. It can be difficult to refuse if the approach comes from the big customer himself. There are two drawbacks to bear in mind most carefully before making a decision on this type of agent:

(*a*)   Can he have unhindered entrée to other big customers who might be his own competitors? (See case history, page 1.)

(*b*)   Is it in his interests, as a purchaser and consumer of the product, to keep its price as low as possible, thereby reducing the profitability of the market? He could complain about a price increase on his own behalf and speak effectively on behalf of the whole market, thus baulking the exporter's plans.

10 Agent / Manager. In some of the less-developed, rapidly changing markets of, say, Africa, the Far East, and Latin America, it is essential for the exporter to have at his disposal a detailed knowledge of the market and a continuous management of his business affairs at a senior level. This is particularly true if the market potential is on a large scale and if the exporter has substantial investment in it.

The answer to this problem is often to appoint a firm to be managing agents or commercial managers. This firm might be a branch of one with a head office elsewhere or a big enterprise in the market in its own right. In Africa, for example, there are French or British merchant firms which have gained expertise in all aspects of commerce there for decades. They are in a position to report on the manufacturer's agents, supervise the exporter's holding in a joint venture, or recommend a new entry into the

24

market or new sales approach as opportunities are seen. They can not only do what the export firm itself would do if it could afford the time and manpower to be constantly on the spot, but in addition, because of their local status, they can lobby authorities to prevent interference. In several instances these managing agents can also offer their own wholesale or retail outlets or distribution networks for marketing the goods.

A common form of payment for the managerial services is a retainer fee plus an agreed share of overall profits in the market as a stimulus to their initiative in developing it.

11 Factory Representative/Agent Controller. Selling agents are best given a tightly defined area of operation, allowing them to concentrate on every possible client on their home ground. But, for the exporter, certain markets group themselves neatly for wider supervision, with one market's experience able to help in developing a neighbouring market and with an importation, sales or servicing base located centrally to serve more than one agent's territory.

It normally causes friction to appoint one agent as a superior or central organiser in a market group. The best solution is to employ a fully salaried "factory representative," often sent out to the post from the exporter's head office. He can reside in any convenient city and can act as organiser, troubleshooter, agency controller, market developer, and general liaison man.

He will not sell to customers, other than accompanying the local agent on key calls. Knowing the parent firm and the local conditions, he is able to make periodic visits back to head office for sales conferences, keeping all parties up to date.

This appointment is especially economical if the parent firm is a group of companies or a multiple-factory firm which is exporting a range of different products to the area through a number of different channels. It would be expensive for specialist salesmen to have to make trips to the agents for each product range.

A factory representative is often located in Cairo for Middle Eastern markets, in Rio de Janeiro or Buenos Aires for South America or in Singapore for South-East Asia. Some groups have a factory representative for EFTA and one for EEC, whilst others locate one in Paris for southern Europe and another in Stockholm for northern Europe. A New York man often looks after the USA, Canada, and Mexico. (See page 136.)

12 Export Management Agency. This type of agent is situated, generally, in the exporter's home country. When the would-be exporter has read this book and thrown up his arms in dismay, he might place the whole business of exporting in someone else's hands and say "Get on with it."

The export management agency acts as the manufacturer's export department, either for all foreign markets or for a selection, complementing the principal's existing arrangements.

He familiarises himself with the manufacturer's programme, facilities, and price structure, investigates potential foreign outlets and exports the maximum on a straight commission basis, or fee plus commission, depending upon circumstances. He might appoint new agents in overseas markets to handle the products or make use of his existing sales channels to funnel the additional lines. He will normally be very conversant with export administration and world market conditions, having had experience handling a long line of goods. His familiarity with specific foreign markets might, however, vary considerably, so it is advisable for the manufacturer to check his record carefully before signing away exclusive rights for each and every market.

The export management agency might well be interested itself in handling the products in its own specific marketing area where it has experience, suggesting other agencies which could take over responsibility for marketing in other territories requiring a special technique.

"Export house" is the modern term for the old established term "export merchant." The new name has been introduced because the old image of a firm just buying in one place and selling at a profit where it could in a foreign market no longer does justice to the wide range of services export houses can offer. They will turn up in various definitions in this book. Many export houses act as export managers, taking over the entire problem from the manufacturer.

When using an export management company, the manufacturer himself still retains the role of principal in all transactions with the foreign customer. However, the export house which offers multiple services might also be willing to provide the manufacturer

26

with the cash to cover the cost of the goods, giving credit to the customer on its own account, taking on the financial risk.

Export management agencies normally sell goods for the manufacturer at the price which would be charged even if there were no such intermediary. This system saves the manufacturer the overheads involved in setting up his own organisation to market the agency's territories and in handling the physical aspects of financial and administrative procedure at home. He merely has to process the orders handed to him as if they were home-based, very often quoting ex works, running no financial risk and not giving credit.

II: AGENT PURCHASING FOR HIMSELF AS PRINCIPAL

13 Export Merchant. Export merchanting is one of the specific activities carried out by what are nowadays termed "export houses" (see previous page). It implies that the merchant purchases the goods from the exporter on his own account as principal. He then resells the goods at a profit to a foreign customer. The merchant thus has the job of finding the customer and taking any financial risk involved in the whole transaction.

The type of agreement that the exporter can have with a merchant firm varies enormously, but generally it ensures that for specified areas the manufacturer will not compete against the merchant by his own sales efforts. The agreement may or may not have a clause to the effect that all orders from the areas not specifically placed by the merchant will be credited to his account with an agreed commission.

The agreement will depend upon the extent to which the manufacturer wishes to encourage the merchant to push his products with special sales promotion. Obviously the merchant is not going to expend his money and efforts promoting in a market which can produce orders which completely bypass him.

If the manufacturer wishes to encourage special efforts from one merchant and yet does not wish to seal off other potential channels (such as smaller but still effective merchants) it has been known for him to keep an "open" market but give an "extra discount to cover promotion" to the main merchant who can spearhead the market.

14 Distributor. Words such as "distributor" or "importer" or "merchant" do not so much describe a particular type of organisation as the *essential nature of a function* which can be performed. There is a great deal of overlapping of these functions and so it is frequently difficult to define an agent as one or the other. But, as stated earlier, knowing that the terms exist and being familiar with their significance can help the exporter to define his own needs when selecting the most profitable form of representation in foreign markets.

The distributor buys from the exporter to resell at a profit. He has, however, exclusive rights to market the goods in his territory. All orders must be channelled through him. To emphasise this, such agents are frequently termed sole distributors or sole concessionnaires, making evident their claim to exclusive rights in the market.

The export merchant might purchase goods from the manufacturer and appoint his own distributors in different areas, giving them the right to resell, or he might act as the distributor himself.

15 Stockist. The stockist either buys direct from the manufacturer or he can be a link further along the chain of marketing. He might buy from the export merchant or from the distributor.

He earns his money by buying and reselling at a profit, but he qualifies for special terms by agreeing to hold special minimum stocks to ensure prompt local supply.

The special terms can be discounts or long credit periods or (very often) the exclusive stockist rights in a definite area. He would not normally stock competitive products.

It is essential to have a network of stockists if the goods are to be promoted widely, so that would-be customers can be told exactly where and when they can obtain supplies.

16 Wholesaler. Although the wholesaler also buys and sells to make his own profit, he has no special agreement with the supplier other than the current terms for each order placed. He can deal in competitive products according to his own judgement of the market requirements. He will place his order either directly with the manufacturer or with any organisation appointed by the manufacturer with sole rights for the area.

17 Trading Company. There are two meanings in the export

28

world for the term trading company. In the broad sense it applies to a firm which buys goods in one market to resell at a profit in another. There are many trading companies with particular know-how in certain markets, usually in very specialised lines of goods, such as furs, textiles, timber, or tea.

They might only have a continuing relationship with the exporter or manufacturer in that they place large-scale orders in advance, providing a guaranteed market. These orders might involve a specification of design or quality which the manufacturer agrees to keep exclusive to the one client in return for the big turnover.

In a more specialised sense, the term trading company describes the unique marketing and purchasing organisations of Japan. That country has developed the system whereby the major part of its exports and imports are handled by a fairly small number of giant firms, expert at all the intricate detail of international trade. They are big enough to have established branches in many parts of the world which now do considerable business between second and third markets. It is therefore possible for a German company to sell to Thailand via a Japanese trading company or for a manufacturer in Peru to sell through one to Britain or America. According to product and market, the trading companies will buy and sell at a profit or act for commission. In many cases, they will note an opportunity for a certain type of product in a market and then, through their network, locate a suitable supply. It is essential to investigate the services of the Japanese trading companies when selling to Japan. (See page 127.)

18 Agents Who Assemble. When East Germany wanted to market its fork trucks in the UK, it looked for the usual type of agent who could sell and service. However, market research showed that there would be a considerable market only if there were widespread facilities for repair and maintenance of the trucks' engines and electrical and hydraulic systems. This would be an expensive operation and there would be the further difficulty of convincing potential customers not only that the trucks worked well and economically, but that the components (unknown in the UK) would give reliable and durable service.

The answer was for the agents, Universal Power Drives Limited, to set up a new organisation, Hustler Fork Trucks, which purchases the East German machines minus engine, hydraulics and electrics. These major components are bought separately from British manufacturers who have designed them to suit this range of trucks. The result is a machine which has been developed for the UK market and which incorporates working parts which can be easily repaired or replaced from convenient local sources. The East German manufacturer exports a substantial number of trucks which, being only a semi-import in their final arrangement, can be sold at economical prices.

In this instance the agent purchases the trucks from the manufacturer and is also the principal when buying the components. He invests his own time and money in re-assembling the machines. His revenue comes from the profit on selling the final product at his own risk.

This type of arrangement can be adopted as the best means of marketing many kinds of equipment overseas. It is the solution to a variety of problems. It makes it possible for the product to be more suitable to local requirements, incorporating a fair amount of local design. It overcomes the obstacles in many markets of very high tariff barriers, allowing a large proportion of the equipment to come from local suppliers. It keeps down prices by benefiting simultaneously from mass production of the basic equipment by the exporter.

19 Sales Agent Who Buys. This category can possibly come under a number of the previous headings. It is added here because it puts a little more stress on the selling responsibilities of the agent, compared with the terms merchant or distributor or stockist. Some successful exporting manufacturers always insist that their sales agents purchase the goods or equipment from them. These are manufacturers who are so sure of their own products and their potential market that they feel they can make the agent pay for the right to represent them.

When the agent has to purchase the products it sorts the keen, confident agent from the man who is just willing to collect an agency in the hope of receiving some orders and the resultant commission. The agent has to be convinced the product is good value and he has to assure himself that the market for it really exists.

When the exporter is in a strong position he can stipulate that the agent becomes the first customer and that if a certain sales target is not reached then he loses the exclusive rights in the territory.

If the agent is good but has not the financial resources to buy expensive products into stock, then the exporter can arrange credit terms of, say, six or twelve months, so that the agent can finance his purchases through his sales. With the date specified for payment staring him in the face he has a powerful incentive to go out and sell.

In return, the manufacturer must agree to keeping delivery date promises scrupulously, maintaining the necessary quality or specification of the product and providing any help required by the agent for staff training and sales promotion.

When it is the sales agent who buys from the manufacturer, then the bad credit risk is greatly reduced. Occasionally purely commission agents can accept orders from clients who are not as creditworthy as they should be. If the client pays the bill, all well and good. If he does not, then perhaps the agent loses the commissions, but the manufacturer has suffered a greater loss. The question of who is responsible for the credit risk and at what point final payment must be covered by special bank arrangements is one which has to be settled at the earliest stages, before an agency agreement has been finally signed.

Thinking of a firm as the sales agent which buys rather than as a distributor or merchant keeps the exporter aware of his own responsibilities in the market. The exporter must always bear in mind that the main aim is to develop the market to its fullest profitability. Selling to the distributor is not the last stage of the process. The agent's rate of progress in the market, his promotional efforts and after-sales service are the concern of the exporter.

III: AGENT ACTING FOR OTHER BUYERS AS PRINCIPALS

It is too easily forgotten that there are buying agents as well as selling agents and that the entrée to a big overseas market is often on your own doorstep.

In London, for example, there is even an association, the Export Buying Offices Association, whose members seek out and purchase more than £50 million worth of goods a year on behalf of a thousand clients in all parts of the world.

In most major trading cities of the world there are branches of international merchants whose principals have asked them to purchase large quantities of goods on their behalf; there are offices or representatives of the Japanese trading companies placing orders for perhaps 70 per cent of all imports into Japan; there are commercial sections of embassies and foreign trade delegations with instructions to locate suppliers of goods and equipment required by their nationalised industries; there are chambers of commerce acting as host to visiting buyers who need to be put in contact with local manufacturers; and there are government offices with details of tenders inviting manufacturers to quote for valuable export orders.

20 Buying Offices.   Many large companies, especially American department stores, cannot just wait for foreign salesmen to call and offer them the high-quality new lines they demand for their own customers. They are obliged to go out in the world and look for the right supplies themselves. They set up buying offices in centres which are most likely to prove happy hunting grounds for new ideas. Their orders can be sufficiently large to provide substantial export business without the need for the manufacturer to visit the particular market. Buying offices place the orders, arrange transport, and see to prompt payment.

21 Buying Houses.   It is usual for buying houses to serve a particular territory or group of territories where they have been established for a long period. Many are the modern development of the former great trading companies which pioneered trade with newly discovered parts of the world. They exported local raw materials from the foreign land and imported any type of goods and equipment needed for local development. They often started manufacturing plants to process raw materials on the spot and had to set up offices in different parts of the world to purchase what they required for all their interests.

As the new territories became independent and more sophisticated, the role of the trading firms changed to suit new conditions, but, generally, their efficient import and export organisation was maintained to meet the new state's needs.

Local industry and commerce found it convenient to use the established international network as a means of locating and buying what they required from abroad.

In this way, the buying houses grew up to serve their specific markets and are deputed to place substantial orders for all kinds of goods, consumer and technical, with manufacturers in many parts of the world.

They combine the jobs of agents and principals, depending upon whether they are ordering for clients as a service or purchasing on behalf of parent or associated companies. They might be free to specify goods at their own discretion or they might be asked to purchase goods as specified by their principals.

22 Buying Agents. Although, again, it may not be possible to differentiate between types of firm by title, because of the overlap of functions, it is as well to mention that there are other companies, termed here "buying agents," which offer the services described in both paragraphs above to a wider range of principals. They seek out suppliers of goods needed by different foreign buyers, they also act as host and documentation clearing house for visiting buyers of many countries in different branches of industry and commerce. Before an exporter embarks on the process of selecting an agent in a particular foreign market, it is certainly advisable to check on these possible export customers based on his home ground. It might well turn out, for example, that his major customers in New Zealand, the USA, West Africa, or Malaysia do most of their buying through agents overseas. This information is readily available with a minimum of desk research, for Board of Trade offices, relevant embassies, and chambers of commerce can usually give a list of buying offices and agents and details of expected visiting delegations, some of which make regular buying tours to purchase or commission goods for coming seasons.

Department stores and fashion houses, big buyers of foreign lines, are very often served by some type of buying house or buying office, one of the main reasons being that they wish to get hold of exclusive lines. This would be more difficult from a sales agent in their own market who would be out to supply as many customers as possible, not just one exclusively.

This often means that a manufacturer can actually lose an export order simply because he has an agent in the market!

A typical occasion was when a Canadian buyer, employed by a big department store, made a trip to London, saw a sample of something he wanted and asked his London buying agent to introduce him to the British manufacturer. But the manufacturer had an exclusive agreement for the Canadian market with a local agent and suggested the buyer deal with him. The buyer was hardly delighted at the thought of having to negotiate the business back in Canada when he was on the spot in London, nor was he at all keen to see the prices burdened with the percentage commission for the agent. He was accustomed to buying in very large quantities and negotiating specially favourable prices direct with the manufacturer on his own ground. The outcome was that the buying agent had to locate an alternative supplier who had no Canadian agent and was thus qualified to receive the order!

It must be remembered that department store buyers are paid to go abroad and buy, and they want to prove the value of their existence by obtaining good prices and securing supplies of exclusive goods.

A buying agent or office will not normally act on behalf of more than one client in any one selling area. If he is looking for goods for one store in Sydney, he will not take on an assignment for a competing store there, but he will be glad to work for a store in Melbourne. If a store in, say, Johannesburg discovers that a competitor has grabbed a nice line in something which is selling very well, then it is likely to contact its own buying agent in the country of origin and ask for a speedy supply of something similar. The buying agent will quite often commission its manufacture if it is not available as standard.

There are many examples of buying agents opening up big new export markets for manufacturers on their own initiative. One London office saw a novelty candle lantern and took a fancy to it. They photographed it themselves and sent pictures to a number of overseas territories. Shortly afterwards an American popped into their office and said he had also taken a fancy to the little novelty. He happened to be a candle distributor! Within a few months the Birmingham maker of the lanterns was working overtime to supply 150 000 of them to the States.

Similarly, a Cornish potter turned a clay error into gold. He accidentally left a hole in a fish's tail which served as handle to a jug. Consequently there was a horrible glug-glugging sound when the jug was used to pour out water. The phenomenon attracted the attention of a buying agent, Dean, Warburg Ltd, who offered the novelty to the USA. The first 10 000 gurgling fishes went down so well, they designed a glugging pink elephant to follow! The American market and others were opened up for the pottery company without the need for the manufacturer to leave Cornwall.

The world's large department stores usually have buying offices or agents in most big European centres, such as London, Paris, Frankfurt, Vienna, Copenhagen, Madrid, Zurich, Brussels, Florence, and Stockholm.

In London there is a subscription circular which, every Friday, lists the names and requirements of buyers from abroad and the buying agent who is acting as host. Called *Overseas Trade News*, one recent sample issue listed 158 buyers from large firms in Dallas, New York, Helsinki, Gothenburg, Brussels, Antwerp, Louisville, Pittsburgh, Newark, Cincinnati, Rochester, Denver, Chattanooga, Philadelphia, Houston, Minneapolis, Boston, Chicago, Toronto, Montreal, Miami, Oakland, Detroit, Indiana, Dayton, Baltimore, Cleveland, Johannesburg, Stockholm, San Francisco, Beirut, Melbourne, Bergen, Tokyo, Sydney, Brisbane, and so on.

These people were all on a tour with substantial budgets for buying and all being looked after on the spot by various buying agents.

A consumer product, especially, can often be test marketed in a very simple way by getting it to be seen by a dozen visiting buyers from stores or supermarkets in the USA, Scandinavia, Japan, and Australia. Their comments, free of charge, can be worth a great deal of market research. One manufacturer, for example, learnt within two minutes that his table mats were too small for the intended market which only bought large sizes. He postponed his intended sales trip, had larger sizes made, and went on a successful tour a little later.

IV: AGENT UNDERTAKING SPECIALISED ASPECT OF EXPORT CYCLE OTHER THAN SELLING

23 Confirming Houses. A confirming house normally acts on behalf of the foreign buyer but is a very valuable asset to the exporting manufacturer. It is, so to speak, the best of both worlds for the exporter, for the confirming house guarantees payment for goods supplied, paying for them on the due date and collecting

35

the cash from the purchaser at a time agreed between the two of them. It is usually the buyer who pays commission to the confirming house for the service, plus any interest if a loan or long credit is involved.

Confirming houses usually include in their service all arrangements for insurance and shipment of the goods to the foreign client.

The transaction, however, is still between the manufacturer and the foreign buyer as principals, with the confirming house acting as an intermediary with subordinate functions. Confirming is often one of the services offered by buying houses.

24 Factors. The steadily expanding use of export factors is an indication of their valuable function. They are, in a way, the counterpart of the confirming house, operating this time for the exporter and not for the foreign buyer.

Theirs is primarily a financial service, for they pay the manufacturer for goods on shipment and then take on the responsibility for obtaining due settlement from the overseas customer. The transaction can be with or without recourse to the manufacturer.

Manufacturers pay a fee to the factors (in the form of a discount on the bills) but they benefit by having more capital available for developing their business instead of waiting for payment from abroad, which at the earliest is usually after the goods have been safely received.

The growth of export factoring shows how competitive international trade has become. Previously only the customers paid (through confirming houses) for the privilege of obtaining foreign goods. Now, through factors, it is the exporter who is paying for the privilege of gaining overseas orders.

25 Shipping and Forwarding Agents. These organisations have existed for a long time and their value will remain for a long time to come. One of the aspects of exporting which frequently terrifies the novice is the thought of all the bother in administration connected with the physical business of transporting the goods from his home country to the foreign buyer anywhere in the world.

All this, including the transport and customs documentation and organisation, the special packing requirements and the customs clearance, can be taken over from the exporter by the shipping and forwarding agents.

Called upon as consultants in export shipping, they can play an important role in gaining export orders, for it is often speedy and prompt delivery which determines where an order should be placed. It frequently requires a lot of know-how when it is a question of working out the best possible means and route to transport goods across the world. The right advice can save money and can cut down on the time to be allowed for transportation.

26 Technical Partnerships. If a farmer in a remote area of Nigeria cannot call for immediate service when his tractor breaks down, he might miss the planting season completely and be without livelihood for a year. It would be uneconomic for every exporter of capital plant to set up servicing facilities for remote Nigerian farmers or similar groups of end users. It is sometimes, however, possible to link up with an existing network of service companies which will take over the maintenance of technical plant in their area and agree to stock spares.

In Nigeria, for example, United Africa Company Group has a subsidiary called UNAMEC which provides a technical service for some manufacturers in special partnership arrangements.

27 Depot Distribution Agents. Similar to the problem of servicing technical equipment is that of warehousing and distributing consumer goods in underdeveloped territories. It is a particularly acute problem for manufacturers of goods which have to be sold through small retail outlets where the proprietors cannot afford to buy in large stocks, but where they expect to be able to call for additional stocks at short notice.

A number of agenting companies are building up special distribution services whereby they maintain depots in many parts of remote territories on behalf of a large number of branded goods manufacturers. They receive large bulk consignments and break them down into smaller stocks for different areas and then make regular deliveries to the smallest local outlets.

This service can be offered on a fee basis, even occasionally on a basis of profit sharing for the development of a market, depending upon the complexity of the service required. Occasionally, for example, with delivery also goes the extra function of cash collection.

These new arrangements can open up markets for manufacturers who would otherwise never dream of attempting to sell there. A separate sales agent can still be the one responsible for promotion, selling-in, bulk importation, and so on, with the distribution company called upon for the use of its depots and local delivery services.

CHAPTER 4

How to Find the Agency Candidates

We once asked an employment service to supply a copy typist. The first job given to her was to type addresses on labels from a list. She typed all the addresses on to the gummed side. She was supposed to be temporary but no appointment was ever so short-lived.

Imagine if we had asked the employment firm to supply a girl for a distant office, where she would have gone on typing on the wrong side of labels for quite a time before we noticed that all mail was being returned because only a blank showed when the address label was stuck on the envelope.

The employment service was supposed to provide secretarial staff which they had personally screened, to save the employers the job of interviewing and testing. What form of test that particular girl had passed we never discovered. During the holiday period temporary staff is in great demand and employment services find the most difficult part of their job is to suck in enough willing people for hiring out. Anyone who qualifies as a girl and knows what a typewriter might look like is possibly suitable for dishing out to the hundreds of short-staffed firms who simply ask for a "temp" to do general office typing.

We did not specify that the girl would be required to type on the non-sticky side of labels. We once were supplied with a girl who wore a hat with an enormous brim and she refused to remove the hat whilst working, so that the other staff in the office were deprived of half their normal share of daylight. Again, we had not specified that the "temp" would be required to work bareheaded.

Perhaps if these two points were to be included in the next request for secretarial help, the employment service might go to the trouble of asking the candidate a few questions on our behalf.

Perhaps our request for girls would be finicky and detailed enough to show in advance that we were not to be lumped with all the other rush of inquiries and served up with the first girl who pops in off the street for some easy money.

It shows that even at such a minor level the person asking for a service must clamour for special attention and must at all times be personally involved in approving the service he is provided with.

As discussed in Chapter 2, the majority of inquiries for foreign representation are so poorly documented that by the time the request has been passed through several hands in an extended chain across the world, any individual answering to the name of "agent" would be considered a suitable candidate to fill the post. If the would-be exporter then appoints the man after only cursory examination by proxy or post, then the chances are that more serious damage than the loss of a few hundred gummed labels would result.

There are many organisations of a variety of types offering free or paid-for services in locating agents in export markets. They can be very helpful if they are used in the right way. To do this the manufacturer must be aware of what service is actually being offered and how the system works which is operating on his behalf. He can then make an intelligent approach for help and make an intelligent appraisal of the results, knowing where the weakness might lie and where the work is incomplete, requiring further efforts on his part.

It is perhaps a help to bear in mind the five stages to the appointment of an export agent. These are:

1   Ensure that the product is exportable (capacity and organisation exist and there are no embargoes)
2   Define the most suitable market
3   Specify the type of agent required
4   Find the agent nearest to the brief
5   Negotiate an effective working agreement with him

It will be seen that most free services deal mainly with only the fourth stage of the process, some having a little to do with the second stage of the process, some having a little to do with the first and third stages. The fifth stage is the real crunch and very few organisations would stick their necks out by attempting to carry it out on the manufacturer's behalf. That is certainly the final move which demands the manufacturer's expertise, knowledge of his own firm and products and assessment of the possibility of creating a satisfactory working relationship with the chosen agent.

When the problem is analysed in this way it becomes clear why so many manufacturers express dissatisfaction with government or other free services in the selection of agents. It is likely that the people offering the help have not sufficiently emphasised the limitations of their helpfulness and the manufacturer has not been sufficiently aware of his own role in filling the gaps.

Now that it has been prefaced with these dire warnings, the list of helpful organisations can follow.

SERVICES OFFERED BY BANKS

The word "banks" is too short to achieve proper significance in this context, especially as it is a term so commonly used in so many other connections. It is probably better to give the title of departments which exist in most big banks everywhere in the world: "Overseas Business Development Section."

Departments with this title or equivalent ones are staffed by commercially orientated executives whose job it is to help clients to open or expand foreign markets.

The word "clients" is also a misnomer, for it does not only mean clients of the bank. The people helped by these sections need not be the bank's customers, in fact the majority appear not to be, and yet no charges are made for an astonishingly comprehensive range of services.

A bank is essential to every trading community. After a baker's shop, a place to drink beer or wine and a funeral parlour, comes the bank. The manager has a pretty good idea of the worthiness (from a business point of view) of almost every citizen and a completely accurate picture of his financial status.

Now all bank managers are interlinked in a highly organised network, on a national and also international scale. Each local community bank is supervised by an area manager, he by a provincial or regional manager and so on up to head office. All banks in any one country have working arrangements with each other for mutual help on behalf of each other's clients, and the banks of one nation are tied by very close-working and friendly relations with the banks of all other nations. There are few, if any, exceptions to this.

Banks have not been slow to appreciate that in addition to their functions as financial stake holders and moneylenders and cash distributors, they have access to every single businessman in the world!

Theoretically they can introduce any businessman to any other businessman and, in practice, they try to do just that when asked.

Some banks have organised this side of their operation more than others. For example, some, like the Australia and New Zealand Bank, invite their customers to have their details registered in a central card index file, giving their type of business and expansion interests. The central file can then be used to effect business introductions between suitable parties. The scope is infinite.

When an exporter in Scotland approaches his own local bank manager for help in finding an agent in Sydney, the manager can forward the inquiry to the business development department of his head office. That department can pass it on to its London office, say, which makes direct contact with the London office of the Australia and New Zealand Bank, which has its own business development department. There the inquiry is screened to see that it is reasonable and that there is some chance for the product on the Australian market; it is then forwarded to the relevant office in Australia.

The central file is consulted and details of the inquiry are sent to the manager of the branch where a likely agent is a customer. This customer is approached personally by his bank manager. If he is willing, then his name and some details about him, including a banker's status report, are sent back to the central office in Australia, back to the office in London, on to the office of the Scottish bank in Edinburgh, say, and through to the local manager who is able to hand over to his customer the name of a willing and possibly suitable agent in Sydney. In fact he will probably have several alternative names to offer.

The customer then is left to make direct contact by correspondence and perhaps by personal visit with the suggested agents, checking up and appointing them in his own way.

This is not such a long-winded operation as this account might make it appear. In many cases there is a short cut, with the local manager putting the client in direct contact with the central business development office, standing to one side himself to avoid over-elongation of the lines of communication. Alternatively, the original inquirer is introduced by his bank to the relevant office of the bank specialising in the foreign territory. In the above example, the Scottish manufacturer could visit the ANZ office in London to discuss his requirements in person.

In addition to pure introductory services, the banks will add their own specialised market advice. The names could come back from Sydney, say, with an added note that the main market for the Scotsman's products would, in fact, be in Western Australia where there is a great deal of new railway construction planned, so that an agent in Perth would be an essential extra or even a recommended alternative. Or the information could come back from Australia that seven manufacturers of similar products have recently set up their own plants in Melbourne, Perth, Brisbane, and Sydney, a procedure which the Scottish firm should consider before going any further.

This type of service can be obtained in the most complex of criss-crossing patterns of contacts for any territory.

First National City Bank, for example, has, apart from 168 offices in the New York Metropolitan Area alone, 241 offices overseas, from Japan, to South Africa, Argentina, Mali, Mauretania, Switzerland, France, Belgium, the UK, etc.

Furthermore, the bank has connections with specialist native banks in every country. Any of its clients can enlist its aid to effect an introduction and the inquiry will be processed through to, if necessary, the merchant in Senegal or Saudi Arabia or Sweden who is willing to be put in touch for business negotiations.

Reciprocally, the manufacturer in Wellington can ask his branch of the National Bank of New Zealand for help in making contact with an agent in New York, and the First National City Bank will on request seek out a suitable firm on its own list of clients to introduce to the New Zealander.

There are many permutations of the service. If the bank which is approached in the export market cannot locate a suitable candidate, it will call on other banks in the area to help. They tend to regard the whole operation as one of good public relations, doing the best possible for the two parties, regardless of allegiance to one bank or another. In the end, all benefit, for an increase in trade produces an automatic increase in banking business. One bank helps another this time and benefits from the good services of another the next time. The approach is totally non-partisan.

Because of the close involvement of banks in all forms of business, both national and international, their intelligence and economic departments have access to enormous quantities of statistics and market development information.

Most major banks publish this information in regular newsletters, specialist surveys and economic digests and bulletins. The latest background information on a market is usually issued to an inquirer requesting help in specific territories.

The Business Development and International Division of Barclays DCO, for example, publishes very detailed economic surveys of its specialist markets compiled from branch managers' reports, so these are based on up-to-date personal know-how. The bank is particularly well informed on little-known territories such as Bahamas, Barbados, Botswana, Lesotho, Guyana, Libya, Malawi, Malta, Sierra Leone, Uganda, Zambia and so on. Important aspects of the economies and trade of these territories are discussed in the bank's "Overseas Review."

Barclays DCO has offices in the UK, the USA, and West Germany, where manufacturers can make personal contact to obtain help in places such as the Leeward Islands or Swaziland. And, of course, the bank's know-how and resources can be called upon by other banks whose interests it represents in those places.

If a customer in California approaches Barclays DCO for introductions to importers in Libya, Uganda, and Ceylon, then the inquiry will be passed straight through to local head offices in Libya and Uganda, where the bank operates, and to a correspondent bank in Ceylon where it is represented by another party. There is thus no problem when it is a matter of "mixing" the territories to include not only the bank's special areas but also areas outside its immediate operations.

A very high proportion of all international trade introductions through banks passes via offices in London. Inside the square mile of the city there are offices of almost every major bank in the world, so that inquiries for Cyprus from Jamaica, from Libya for Poland, from San Francisco for Nigeria, from Hamburg for Trinidad are most likely to be fed in and out of London en route for their destination. Another big centre of this trade information traffic is Paris, especially where it concerns former French dependencies in different parts of the world. Political changes have had surprisingly little effect upon banking channels which follow the well-worn courses created by decades of regularly flowing business.

The one document common to all material transmitted from bank to bank during these trade inquiries is the banker's status report. This is necessarily attached to information concerning the firm or individual initiating the inquiry. When a suitable agent or importer is located, a status report about him is included in the material which is sent back.

Samples of typical specimen status reports are shown in Appendix 2. They were prepared for this book by a famous international bank and are representative of the type of reports reproduced by most other banks. They show a good report, a moderately good report, and a third which can be regarded as a warning concerning credit.

Because status reports are so essential to a bank's operations, it is necessary for manufacturers to make trade inquiries through their bank when approaching an outside bank for specialised help. No one will make a move until the manufacturer's status report has been delivered.

However, if possible, manufacturers should try to insist that they have personal contact with the outside bank with specialised know-how, otherwise there is the grave danger that an inadequate briefing will produce the wrong results. If, for example, your own bank is passing the inquiry on to BOLSA, the Bank of London and South America, because the inquiry concerned, say, Argentina, Brazil, or Chile, it would be advisable to arrange to be put in touch, either by correspondence or personal visit, with one of the BOLSA offices in the UK or the USA or France or Switzerland so that discussions around your problem can fill out a proper picture of your needs and the likely way to meet your requirements in Latin America.

Making personal contact with foreign banks after an official introduction is not so difficult, no matter where you are situated, for the interlinking of services is highly organised and very comprehensive. Banks are improving their coverage especially to help international traders by new groupings to expand the sharing of facilities and know-how. An excellent example is

Intercontinental Banking Services Limited which was formed in February 1968 by Barclays Bank, Lloyds Bank, National Bank of New Zealand, Australia and New Zealand Bank, Bank of London and South America, Barclays Bank DCO, and the Chartered Bank. Together, these banks have an economic intelligence network provided by 3000 overseas branches. Ordinary trade and agency inquiries are still to be handled by each individual bank, but this sort of joint organisation is an indication of the breadth of the services which can be called upon.

Merchant banks and finance houses are also grouping into international networks for the purpose of expanding credit and financial advisory services for exporters engaged in bigger and ever more complex international projects. These moves also open up wider services for other types of economic and trade information, including the introduction to each other of suitable business partners in different parts of the world. An example is the Amstel Club, an association of leading financial institutions from Austria, Belgium, Denmark, Finland, France, West Germany, Holland, Italy, Norway, Portugal, Spain, Sweden, Switzerland, the UK, and the USA.

Advantages of Banks. Introductory services offered by banks are completely free of charge. They are also quite speedy in operation. A manufacturer can expect to start receiving suggested names and addresses of possible agents within three weeks even from the other side of the world, and much more quickly if the territories are closer.

If there is any need for urgent action, then the banks are willing to initiate inquiries by cable, sometimes asking for a contribution to cover the additional expense, but often providing this service free of charge too.

Because of the intimate knowledge banks have of their own territories, they can very rapidly let a manufacturer know if his plans to market there are completely off-beam or if there is any chance at all of finding the type of agent he has described.

Because banks primarily consist of branches, each serving a very specific local community, inquiries can be very accurately directed, when necessary, to a single city or province. It is possible to ask for an agent not only in Europe, or the UK, but in Leeds or Manchester; not merely in the USA but in Detroit or Los Angeles;

not just in South Africa but in Durban or Capetown; or in any combination of narrowly defined areas.

Furthermore, as each recommendation comes back from the agent's own bank manager, there is the invaluable combination of a personal introduction via a reliable and impartial man of commercial experience.

Shortcomings of Banks. This is not intended to imply criticism of the introductory services offered by the banks, but rather to stress again that they do not amount to anything like a comprehensive agent selection service. They are no substitute for a proper market research programme, although they would definitely contribute valuable material to such a programme. If the new agent is expected to open up a big new market, then the bank's introduction is no substitute for a personal meeting with the agent to work out a complete business relationship. The banks will accept no part of the process of drawing up the best type of agency contract, which requires legal consultation.

The banks may not be in a position, because of the specialised products being handled, to be able to make any assessment of the type of agent best suited to the marketing approach.

Lastly, and very important, banks are definitely geared to appraisals of an agent's financial status and not his selling ability. This vital aspect of a candidate has to be judged by other means.

Just imagine, by walking into one's own bank manager's office, it is possible to tap the expertise of Chase Manhattan, Westminster Bank, the Hong Kong and Shanghai Banking Corporation, Kansallis Osake Pankki of Finland, the Standard Bank of Africa, Fuji Bank of Japan, Bank of Montreal, Bank of New South Wales (the full list amounts to 700 pages in the *Banker's Almanac*!). It is a free service worth bearing in mind next time you are looking for an agent.

SERVICES OFFERED BY CHAMBERS OF COMMERCE

Many interweaving threads go to make up the pattern of international industry. There are the banks, as discussed previously, and, fulfilling different functions, there are the chambers of commerce. These, too, are linked on a world-wide scale, offering special facilities for the introduction of a firm in one country to a potential business partner in another country.

The importance and influence of a chamber of commerce vary according to its size and the sort of community it serves, but in some territories the chamber of commerce fulfills many of the duties which, in other areas, would be the responsibility of the government, acting almost as a department of commerce or a trade ministry.

Through chambers of commerce there is a network joining together the majority of the world's trading firms, and this network can be put at the disposal of members for the purpose of locating an agent to serve their interests in a foreign market.

The London Chamber of Commerce, for example, has an "Agency System," which operates on behalf of British firms seeking overseas agents and also on behalf of foreign firms wishing either to find UK agents or UK principals.

Information about would-be foreign sales agents is published by the Chamber in its "Digest" and circulated to members. Information can also be included about foreign manufacturers in need of British representation.

Conversely, details about a British firm's requirements can be submitted to a corresponding chamber of commerce in a foreign country, where it will be published in its local newsletter or other publication or where investigations will be made to locate a suitable candidate to be agent.

A search can be initiated on a national scale, or, where desired, it can be directed to a specific town or province through a local chamber.

In addition, there are other types of international chambers formed to encourage and facilitate trade between two particular markets. There is the American Chamber of Commerce (United Kingdom) in London, and the Anglo-Israel Chamber of Commerce, the Belgian Chamber of Commerce in London Incorporated and similar two-country chambers in most major trading centres such as New York, Hamburg, Düsseldorf, Paris, Brussels, Johannesburg, Sydney, Montreal, and Amsterdam. They can provide direct introductions to possible agents and, at the same time, they can be a valuable source of background information on marketing methods and the state of the particular country's economy.

A service they can provide which can be of exceptional value in some instances is to introduce exporters to those local firms which are already doing good regular business with the territory in question; firms which are most probably leading members of the special chamber (or of the relevant country section of the ordinary chamber of commerce).

It is often feasible to share a good overseas agent with a firm exporting related products which are sold to a similar market but are not in fact competitive. This can be a speedy method of locating a highly recommended agency which has already proved itself in the field for another exporter.

The advantage of finding agents through a chamber of commerce is that the names put forward (on both sides) can generally be assumed to be reliable firms, with nothing known to the chamber to blemish their reputation. It is a form of personal recommendation of reliability.

However, the same limitations exist as those already stressed. The introduction is no guarantee that the firm is the right kind of agent for the business to be handled nor that the market is a key one for the product. If an inadequate briefing is given to the chamber, then unsuitable agents can be proposed. And after the introduction, it is up to the two parties to make their own agreement on all practical matters of business. A suggested name from a chamber is by no means the signal for immediate appointment.

CUSTOMERS' RECOMMENDATIONS

In the preceding section, it was suggested that chambers of commerce could make introductions to successful exporters of allied products who might be willing to share overseas representation where there was no element of competition.

In the same way, a manufacturer could think of locating the best agent by approaching existing or potential big customers in a foreign market and asking their advice about local agents and importers.

In selecting an agent one is concerned with two aspects of the business cycle—the relationship between the manufacturer and

49

the agent and the relationship between the agent and the customer. It is possible to reach the right agent in the middle by working from either end.

It is necessary to be on guard in case the customer who is approached suggests that he himself could easily take over the extra function of agent for the rest of the market. He very possibly would not have access to his own competitors who might make up the remaining section of one's market. But the customer's recommendation (or preferably the recommendation of several customers) could avoid a lot of wasted effort and could pinpoint a likely agent who would already have the entrée to important clients.

The danger exists, of course, that if the customer mentions a name, then that firm might already be handling competitive products, the reason why the customer already knows the firm. At least this will give an indication of the strength of the competition and there is always the chance that the agent can be inclined to take on a new supplier if for some reason he is seriously dissatisfied with his existing principal.

Alternatively, the manufacturer can approach customers of related products to ask for recommendations of local agents. In this way there could be a direct lead to a good agent who is keen to take on lines complementary to those he is currently handling. Perhaps the man distributing someone's electric irons will be happy to take on someone else's ironing boards. Or the electric relay stockist might well expand his business profitably with an imported line of solenoid valves.

FEDERATIONS OF AGENTS

The growth of competition in international trade has increased the importance of the agency business. Agents know this and they also appreciate that the steady untroubled growth of their profession will depend upon the extent to which they can regulate their business procedure and methods. Accordingly, in most major markets the agents have formed themselves into official bodies to control their industry.

In Amsterdam there are the headquarters of the International Union of Commercial Agents and Brokers. Its members are organisations of commercial agents and representatives in Belgium,

Britain, France, Germany, Israel, Italy, the Netherlands, Scandinavia (the Federation of Nordic Commercial Agents, Oslo, which has its own member associations in Denmark, Finland, Norway, and Sweden), Switzerland, and the United States of America. The aims of the IUCAB are worth reproducing. They are:

1   To promote the profession of agent and broker
2   To promote the responsibility and prestige attached to this profession
3   To promote contacts between principals and agents in different countries
4   To promote international trade

Its activities are therefore described as:

1   Co-ordinating the work of national associations of agents and brokers
2   Giving guidance to the formulation of the duties and responsibilities of the agent and broker
3   Stimulating international meetings of sectional groups —for example, foodstuffs, textiles, machinery, and so on—to discuss problems in their specific field
4   Organising international congresses

The Union claims a total membership through the affiliated associations of over 50 000 agents and it sees as one of its functions the introduction of principals to suitable agents.

The main way in which this is achieved is through the medium of the publication which each association distributes to its members.

The German journal is called *Der Handelsvertreter und Handelsmakler* (literally "The Commercial Agent and Broker") and it is the fortnightly official organ of the Centralvereinigung Deutscher Handelsvertreter- und Handelsmakler-Verbände (CDH). This is itself a federation of the twelve German provincial or Land associations and twenty-four federal trade associations, representing agents in every branch of industry and commerce. It claims to encompass about 30 000 members.

The Manufacturers' Agent is the title of the monthly journal published by the Manufacturers' Agents' Association of Great

Britain and Ireland Incorporated. This organisation was founded as long ago as 1909. One of its many services is the issuing of standard forms of agreement between manufacturers and agents for British or foreign representations and advice on all matters connected with these.

Notices and advertisements in these publications inform agents of opportunities for representing Austrian toys, French electrical fittings, animal hair and garden swings, Yorkshire rainwear, Spanish canned fish, and Australian kitchen gadgets.

The various associations of agents publish directories of their membership which can be purchased by manufacturers. A list of the addresses of each association appears in Appendix 5.

Britain is, we believe, unique in having a separate privately organised register, the BAR (British Agents Register). This has been set up as a service to all manufacturers seeking representation in the UK for local or imported goods.

It publishes a monthly subscription journal called *British Agents Review* which carries a considerable amount of advertising seeking agents for products from many parts of the world. A recent issue offered Italian washing machines, Austrian woodworking equipment, French industrial expansion joints, Belgian trousers, Danish carpets, Dutch colour cards, Swedish paper products, South African food and animal foods, and Canadian theatrical make-up.

It is interesting to note that almost all the announcements for foreign goods were placed in the name of the trade sections of the countries' embassies or specialised chambers of commerce in London. This is evidence of the activity of those organisations described in other sections of this chapter.

A remarkable extra service offered by British Agents Register is an agency list selection broken down into 2700 categories. These are classified according to type of outlets visited, under the four major headings of Retailers, Wholesalers, Trade (professional and industrial), and Manufacturers. It is therefore possible to obtain from BAR a list of agents calling on cafés, cutlery retailers, wallpaper retailers, or tobacconists; or on wholesalers of musical instruments, photographic goods, or wine and spirits; or agents selling to accountants, hospitals, or education authorities; or agents visiting cycle manufacturers, tailors, and stationery printers.

If desired, lists can also be supplied according to the area of

Britain covered by the agent, broken down into ten regions, such as London, Southern Home Counties, Western Counties, South Wales, Ireland, Scotland, etc. BAR charges a fee for the supply of these lists. (See address, Appendix 5.)

GOVERNMENT DEPARTMENTS

The British Government has now chosen to call its trade attachés at foreign embassies "Commercial Diplomatic Officers." It is a change of name following a change of emphasis, for greater efforts are being made to give on-the-spot help to British exporters seeking to open new markets.

The same is true of most other countries' governments, because international trade is nowadays one of the keystones of government policy in times of peace. It is now much more difficult than it used to be to divide the world into the producers on one side and the buyers on the other, for even the least developed nations are setting up their own industries either to convert their own local materials into more finished goods to earn a greater level of foreign exchange, or to meet more of their own local needs to reduce spending on foreign imports.

Countries are competing, if not in arms, then in standards of living, and political or ideological success is being measured in terms of possessions. Countries have to export more in order to be able to afford to import more.

Accordingly, ambassadors, foreign ministers, and premiers or presidents, as well as officials of the trade ministries, are more and more seeing themselves as salesmen or promotional managers for their countries' exports.

Exporters might as well take advantage of this energetic activity. After all, the costs are being met by public funds to which firms are contributing through taxes.

Export Intelligence, the Board of Trade organisation which aids and advises exporters, handles about 50 000 export inquiries per month, a large proportion of these being requests for help in finding overseas agents. This side of the service is highly organised. A special form, entitled "Agency Inquiry," asks about forty questions of the firm seeking an agent. These cover details of the firm's export management organisation, its size and turnover, the type of agency required, the sort of qualifications the agent should have, the degree to which the proposed market has already been covered or researched.

The intention is to produce as detailed a pen-picture as possible of the whole problem so that the overseas officer can use his judgement to pick out the most suitable candidates. The completed questionnaire, with any possible additional information including catalogues, prices and sales literature, is sent to the Commercial Diplomatic Officer in the relevant territory. He makes local inquiries and if he finds interest in the matter expressed by a possible agent, he sends back to the firm in the UK a written report on the candidate with notes on his commercial standing, general ability, sales strength, and business set-up. Information is given on whether the agent carries stocks, the type of client he sells to, and how many salesmen are employed.

The approach is business-like. Neither the Board of Trade nor the officers overseas will simply provide a list of agents, as the intention is to pick people exactly suited to the job in hand.

Naturally, the selection is only as good as circumstances will allow it to be—it depends upon the adequacy of the initial briefing given by the manufacturer. If the type of agent or the scope of the market for the product is not correctly defined, then the final choice may prove to be unsuitable. Furthermore, the Commercial Diplomatic Officer cannot be a specialist in every type of product. He can only act on the manufacturer's behalf within the limitations of his own experience, although he will call upon any other available specialists where this can be done conveniently.

The officer's report cannot, either, take into account the financial standing of the agent, which must be checked separately through a bank, nor can he negotiate a contract on behalf of the manufacturer. The most he can offer in that respect is an introduction to a local lawyer if necessary, with a slight briefing on any special local legislation requirements.

As with other similar services, the manufacturer is not in a position to control the effort being made for him, nor can he be too insistent upon the way things are handled. However, it is a service from which many exporters have benefited and it is not a bad thing to have one's local embassy lending a hand. The officials there can be mines of information on many aspects of the country in which they are located and, in a continuing relationship, they can be most helpful in introducing the exporter and his agent to a very wide range of contacts at a high level.

INDUSTRIAL OR TRADE ASSOCIATIONS

The majority of well-organised trade associations or industrial confederations have set up export advisory sections. These can frequently be of assistance in finding agents by making contact with their opposite numbers in the relevant territories. For example, associations of machine tool firms often have memberships consisting of manufacturers and also importers. They also publish some form of regular bulletin or newsletter which can draw their members' attention to foreign importers who wish to act as agents for additional ranges, or to foreign manufacturers who are seeking agents. These associations are very willing to "take in each other's washing," extending their services to the international as well as the national plane.

The co-operation exists on a multi-level criss-crossing pattern. Associations for identical industries communicate with each other; also associations can make contact with their counterpart which acts for the complementary side of the industry. That is, the association for electrical manufacturers could make contact in another country with the association for electrical wholesalers or the association for electrical contractors, asking for help in introducing a member to a suitable trading partner.

If the exporter has been able to create an accurate portrait of the type of firm which would most suit him as an agent, then his association can be especially helpful in putting him in touch with a group of firms relevant to his needs. It is often a surprise to discover what associations do exist, so that instead of laboriously beating through directories (90 per cent wasted effort usually) or putting a net out over a very wide industrial area, one can be linked immediately with a whole herd of the game one is seeking.

How many people, in Britain or abroad, for example, know that in London alone there are associations of Boiler Setters, Chimney and Furnace Constructors; Manufacturers of Agricultural Chemicals; Plywood and Veneer Manufacturers; Roofing Felt Manufacturers; Theatre Technicians; Clothing Contractors; not only Consulting Engineers, but also Consulting

Scientists; Crane Makers; Distributors to Self-Service and Coin-Op Laundry and Allied Trades; Fishing Tackle Makers; Gut Processors; Marine Traders; Oriental Carpet Traders; Paper and Board Exporters; Printing Machinery Importers; Road Traffic Sign Makers; Tar Distillers; Underwater Contractors . . . to mention only a selection?

The secretariats of these organisations are usually very willing to receive details of attractive business proposals and make them known to the membership. Once more, the simpler it is the more specific one has been in research. It is better, for example, to go direct to the sub-group of lorry-mounted crane firms than to spread the effort over all mechanical handling companies.

PROFESSIONAL CONSULTANTS

The services mentioned up to this point have all implied a considerable amount of work on the part of the manufacturer seeking the agent. Referring back to page 40, in the five-stage process of appointing agents, the initial appraisal of the manufacturer's organisation for export and his products, the overall research to define key markets and the creation of a brief to make the most of these through the chosen agents have all remained the manufacturer's own sole responsibility. The other services have been more in the nature of bloodhounds, chasing after the quarry when the manufacturer has given them the right scent and pointed their noses in the right direction.

Although a large number of manufacturers are expert at their job of making their products they might not be in a position to do a critical self-analysis for export or a penetrating research survey of potential overseas markets. They might in fact not have the spare time or executive manpower to do this.

As export markets are becoming so essential nowadays to the survival of a growing number of manufacturers, the market research and marketing consultancy firms are setting themselves up to meet the new need for research which cuts across national boundaries. This is being achieved by either forming reciprocal working agreements with market research firms in other countries or, in the major markets, by forming their own subsidiaries.

It is surprising that in the past (and in the present!) so many manufacturers have spent considerable sums in ensuring the correct research has been done on their home market but have been reluctant to spend anything at all in researching world markets. And the world outside can so often increase turnover by 20 or 30 per cent for much less effort than it would take to increase the home market by even half that amount. But the facts (see page 8) are there to be seen—so many manufacturers who are so professionally efficient in their approach to the home market wander into export markets like amateur explorers.

But things are likely to change on this score, because marketing consultants are expanding their international services which in turn should create a bigger demand, making export research, we hope, snowball towards the size of home market research.

Market research companies have their own professional associations, ESOMAR, situated in Switzerland, with representatives looking after its interests in a number of other countries. Inquiries for international research to the association will be answered with a list of the members in most major countries, so that the manufacturer can select the most convenient firm.

CEREC (Compagnies d'Experts en Recherche Economique) is a trading consortium of market research firms specialising in industrial and commercial work. It has member firms in France, Italy, Germany, Benelux, Switzerland, and Britain. The head office of CEREC is in Lausanne, Switzerland. What is more, the individual member firms of the consortitum have their own network of international associates or subsidiaries. One of these, for example, Industrial Market Research Limited of London, has daughter companies or affiliates in over thirty different countries, from Japan to Mexico, from Scandinavia to East and West Africa.

PA International is another new grouping of marketing and research companies. It has daughter companies in the UK, France, Germany, Italy, Spain, Greece, Belgium, and the Scandinavian countries and, further afield, in Australia, New Zealand, South-East Asia, etc. The latest office has been opened in Los Angeles, California.

Within the PA group a new division has been formed called PA International Marketing which has as its prime objective the assistance of manufacturers who wish to expand their marketing into new territories.

Management Selection Limited set up a subsidiary in partnership with International Trade Information called MSL Export Services Limited. This made use of affiliates and subsidiaries in most European countries, in the Far East, and in the USA to research local markets, seek out potential agents, and introduce manufacturers to a short-list of the best candidates.

One of the main advantages stressed by these international consultants is the employment of local experts wherever possible to do the field work. They have facilities for research in the German market to be done by German researchers, for reports from Australia to be written by Australian specialists. In the less sophisticated markets, surveys are often carried out by local interviewers or economists under the supervision of a trained researcher sent out specially for the job.

Each of the firms can provide all or any part of the whole agency selection process, from an appraisal of the production capacity of the manufacturer, his system of costing and pricing to a definition of his key markets, the detailed profile of the best type of agent and personal interviews with candidates in order to short-list them.

PA International Marketing go even further. They are able to take on the supervision of a marketing programme in an export territory on a continuing basis. They can keep the agent motivated, on his toes. They can regularly re-assess targets and performance and report on new market opportunities. The agent would be supervised by the associate or subsidiary company of the group in his area and the manufacturer would liaise with his own local office.

One benefit of this type of expert supervision, not only of an agent but of the market as a whole, is that an assessment can be made at the proper time about the advisability of founding a local branch factory or entering into a joint manufacturing project. These are moves which are often delayed too long because it is not in the interests of the agent to suggest them and the manufacturer usually visits a foreign market comparatively rarely and for short periods. The specialist consultant on the spot has all the facilities for maintaining a constant watch over the exporter's interests.

On a recent project, PA International Marketing had to survey the whole of Europe for a manufacturer. They worked out that the spare capacity in the client's plants could warrant the pricing of export production on only a marginal increase of overheads. On the manufacturer's behalf they selected agents and gave each a market briefing. Within a period of only ten months the manufacturer's overall sales had increased by 25 per cent, the extra coming entirely from new export markets.

At that stage the consultants did another costing analysis. They worked out the cost of an expansion programme to increase production capacity, a new pricing policy to take this into account and a new marketing approach to meet the changing situation.

Turnover rapidly grew and the management of the firm did not have too much of an extra burden to shoulder.

Another example can be given by Associated Industrial Consultants, a group of companies offering specialist help to exporting manufacturers.

There was a firm, T and W Lees (Associated British Hats) of Stockport, Cheshire, making fur hats and hoods, whose business had been hit by the epidemic which destroyed so many rabbits in the UK. They had to import rabbit fur, forcing up the price of their goods. AIC were called in and initially advised that half the factory should be leased off and production increased by more intensive use of the remaining half.

Then new markets had to be developed overseas. For a fee of £500 ($1200) AIC did a world survey to select the most likely markets and then, for a fee of £900 ($2160) they did a special survey in depth of one market—Finland.

A researcher personally visited Finland, taking samples of the client's products, his export price lists, and a draft agreement which indicated the terms of business which the client was willing to agree with a suitable agent.

The consultant brought back descriptions of the types of hats popular in Finland, details of retail prices and discounts, an analysis of the value of advertising in the market and the market shares held by leading brands.

On his advice, the manufacturer was able to appoint an agent who had connections with a big department store and whose managing director was president of the Finnish wholesalers' association.

The client had to make up his own mind about the value of the findings and the decision to take for the future. He decided to follow the recommendations and push export sales. In less than three years his export sales rose from 33·9 to 51·9 per cent of total sales. His share of all hat exports from the UK rose from 3·9 to 8·7 per cent. He opened up the Finnish market for the first time and trebled existing sales to Western Germany. His exports increased to Austria, Switzerland, and Australia.

The advantage implicit in using consultants for the selection of agents and the opening up of overseas markets is that the client can agree a brief and see that this is kept to strictly. Paying the piper, the client can call the tune, seeing that he gets satisfactory service. Furthermore, he can benefit from the accumulated experience of the consultants who are researching foreign markets and selecting agents all the time, not just once or twice in a generation, which would be true of the manufacturer himself.

The disadvantage, of course, is that the manufacturer has to pay for the service, but, when his management time and travel expenditure which would otherwise have to be spent are taken into account, this is not so significant. It is worth paying for the right to demand satisfaction.

CHAPTER 5

Picking, Prodding, and Appraising the Agent

The old saying was that marriage came first and love surely followed. Few take that point of view nowadays. The modern method is to select one's own partner. There is less and less being left to trust, or chance.

Perhaps exporters think that separation is easier from business partners. Whatever the reason, too many manufacturers enter too lightly into relationships with their overseas partners. They should take a few lessons from the youth of today and personally make sure that they are making the right choice before it is too late. Separations are costly in time and money.

PERSONAL VISIT, QUESTIONNAIRE, AND DESK RESEARCH

No matter how the agent has been located, through any of the "marriage bureaux" described in the previous chapter, the manufacturer himself should vet the short-listed candidates. A personal interview will have three beneficial effects:

1   Allow each party to decide whether a working arrangement is feasible
2   Provide the occasion for a fully detailed discussion of the product and the market
3   Stimulate the agent to work for a real person, not just a name on some notepaper

When appointed to develop the manufacturer's market, the agent is like a tenant on his estate. He is not likely to make the maximum effort on behalf of an absentee landlord.

Even if it is impossible for the exporter to make a personal visit to interview agents on their home ground, then the least he can do is to telephone them and go over as many points as possible in a direct, personal conversation. The longest-distance phone call from Europe to Japan, or Edinburgh to Auckland, does not cost more than the price of entertaining a local agent to a business dinner.

Before getting in contact it is valuable to prune the short-list or brief oneself on the candidates by correspondence. One way is to send an identical questionnaire to each potential agent. The replies will give a lead to the most likely prospects and will allow the manufacturer to check salient points in the later personal discussion.

The questionnaire will vary according to circumstances, but the following is an idea of how some successful exporters have interrogated agents by correspondence:

1   When was the agency founded?
2   Names and ages of senior executives
3   Names and ages of salesmen
4   What other agencies are held?
5   What is the turnover per principal (or average)?
6   Average size of order from customers
7   How many customers are visited regularly?
8   How many calls per month per salesman?
9   How often is each customer seen per annum?
10   Which areas are realistically covered?
11   What selling points are seen for my product?
12   What obstacles are foreseen on your market?
13   How much should be spent on promotion?
14   Which market factors should still be researched?
15   What forms of promotion might be employed?
16   What stocks are you willing to hold?
17   What servicing arrangements are available?
18   What means of transport are at your disposal?
19   Membership of trade associations
20   Name of bankers

Strengths and weaknesses can quickly come to light when agents are obliged to fill in answers to questions like these. It also indicates that the principal means business. An agent unwilling or unable to give satisfactory replies is better off the short-list at an early stage. The keener, more dynamic agent will be pleased to expound upon the answers, taking the opportunity to show his know-how and efficiency.

Naturally, not all the facts and figures can be taken at face value. Spot checks should be made to assess the degree of exaggeration, modesty, or dishonesty which has flavoured the response. There are many sources for verification. These include the commercial officer at the local embassy, who can supply a report on the standing and reputation of the agent; the bank manager, who can arrange for a status report from the financial point of view, issued by the agent's bank to the exporter's bank; the agent's own chamber of commerce or trade association, preferably through the exporter's own equivalent organisation.

In addition it is advisable to get in touch with one or other of the agent's existing principals and one or two of his major customers. This should be done with the agent's knowledge. It would be strange if he objected to anyone checking his references.

This "desk research" can be conducted quite speedily (especially if telex is used) at negligible cost of effort or cash and yet at the end of it the manufacturer will have gone a long way in assessing the relative merits of the various candidates. Then should come the personal visit or the telephone conversation to obtain a feel of the other party's character and attitude.

It is important that the assessment should be made by someone at the manufacturer's end who has the authority to say yes to the final appointment. It is absolutely vital, if a foreign trip is made to interview the agents, that the person going should be of the most senior rank, competent to negotiate an agreement and amend or cancel draft provisions and sign a contract.

He must be sure of returning with an agent definitely having been signed on, otherwise it would have been a costly venture. That is why the detailed preparation of the short-list is so important. Without it the trip can be a wild goose chase, or, even worse, an exporter can find himself signing on an unsuitable candidate simply because he cannot afford to make a second trip later! (There have been many instances of this.)

The questionnaire and the subsequent spot checking will automatically raise some queries and the exporter can go into a meeting knowing which aspects of the agency he needs to investigate further and which possible fears he needs to have allayed or verified, for example:

1   Is the agency firm too big? Will his product be left to fend for itself instead of being pushed personally?
2   Is the agency too small, so that his clients will not receive an adequate service in outlying areas?
3   Is the agency in decline? Are the senior personnel content just to tick over, having lost the initial drive when the agency was founded?
4   Is the agency on the way up? Will this mean that he can tap the rocketing energy to boost his sales? Will there be too many additional accounts picked up to swamp the agency, or is growth to be planned and controlled?

It is always a sound idea, for any meeting, to prepare the facts and figures *in advance* so that discussion time can be devoted to settling doubts. If the meeting is taken up with a factual briefing, then there is little time available for the participants to exercise judgement. They are too involved absorbing detail.

SUPPORT AND TRAINING

An official at the Board of Trade said "Good agents are not found, they are made." He also went on to suggest that good agents can be turned into bad agents if starved of the right support. This means that government and other organisations can help to locate the right type of agent, but it is up to the manufacturer to maintain the right relationship in order to ma e the most of the services the agent is able to offer.

Agents are keen to make profits. If a manufacturer does not provide the backing for his sales efforts, then this not only spoils the market for the product, but it also has the doubly vicious effect of forcing the agent to devote himself to other principals who are willing to co-operate more with him. The lax manufacturer then has to overcome those handicaps if he wishes to retrieve lost ground.

Because an export agent is by definition working remotely from the centre of a manufacturer's activities, away from the sales headquarters and the production plant, he is all the more dependent upon conscious efforts made to keep him up to date on background data, new developments, and future plans. In the home market, with generally more frequent contact amongst personnel, there are informal, organic channels of communication.

In the export field, if nobody organises official and regular means of communication, then the agents simply remain uninformed—and this is almost synonymous with uninvolved.

For this reason it pays to spend a little on the production of a newsletter or international bulletin to be distributed to foreign representatives. It can consist of formal announcements of new products, price changes, staff appointments, with the addition of sales news of contracts, installations, satisfied customers, as well as a seasoning of more personal news about export staff or company achievements in overseas markets.

The newsletter can encourage a cross-fertilisation of news and ideas from agent to agent by publishing contributions submitted by the agents. These can cover sales methods, new techniques in promotion, personal announcements and, very valuable, comments on the local economic situation. It is usually of very great interest for businessmen to read the personal assessment of market trends from counterparts in different territories.

Newsletters, rather than house magazines, are effective because they are topical, personal, little trouble to produce and very inexpensive. They can actually cost less than individual letters from different departments to a number of foreign agents. They act as a constant reminder that the principals exist as living, working partners, so that there is a steady incentive to cooperate.

Nowadays the very cheap forms of copying and offset printing, offered as services from outside or available internally in even very small firms, make it possible to enliven a newsletter with photographs of personnel, diagrams of layouts and cuttings from newspapers. The impact on representatives across the waters or over the mountains is out of all proportion to the negligible time it takes to prepare them.

There is a double-sided impact, because regular communication of this kind not only keeps the principal in the forefront of the agent's attention—it also acts as a constant reminder to home-based people that they have agents to support. The demands of everyday local business problems make it difficult, an act of determined willpower, to bear the foreign agents in mind. A regular newsletter deadline ensures that export markets, too, come periodically to mind, getting at least a share of the office's attention.

One firm in the UK has agents in many countries, including Japan, Switzerland, the USA, Canada, Sweden, Germany, and Italy. The best known agent is the one who himself sends a copy of his own newsletter to head office! He is not producing the biggest turnover, but he seems to enjoy the best, most personal support from London.

The sense of the agent's personal involvement with the principal's plans should be a prime objective in all dealings with export markets. This is especially true when preparing sales literature. So much waste occurs when the manufacturer simply runs off extra quantities of a leaflet for overseas distribution. Unexpected parcels arrive at the agent's office and these are duly stored away, to be thrown out when a new supply is received to replace them.

Sales literature is usually produced to coincide with a particular event in the home market—a big promotional drive or an exhibition. Its arrival overseas may not be a convenient moment for a parallel action by the agent. The literature may not even be entirely suitable for his market, stressing perhaps the wrong sales points or, sorry to have to say this, in the wrong language or in a mistranslation of the original.

Sales literature is "literature" to the people who have created it but "give-aways" or "hand-outs" to those who receive parcels of it. The art is to make the agent feel he has helped to create it. Get him to invest something of his own in the material and he will be reluctant to let it collect dust on his shelves.

An effective technique is to provide proofs of proposed leaflets or catalogues at an early stage. Run off the illustrations and any colour work in quantity, leaving a gap for the text. Add the text when the agent has submitted his own translation or amended copy.

He can be chased for the translation to meet a deadline. When the finished material arrives he will be all the keener to use it, for it will be partly the result of his own efforts if he has done the translation, or of his own investment if he has had to pay for a translation. It also gives him a chance to decide in advance how many copies he requires. Some firms supply a given quantity free of charge and ask a moderate contribution to costs for additional copies. This again prevents waste and yet gives the keen agent a chance to do some promotion at an economic price.

Implied in "involvement" is "regular contact." Telephone conversations should be encouraged between home-based executives and the overseas agent. The voice produces a much more intimate co-operation than a letter. Telex should be used rather than letter, not only for speed but because again the direct link reinforces the feeling of being closely connected with each other's activities.

Best of all, indispensable to any really successful agent-principal relationship, is the personal visit. Very few principals can honestly claim to visit their agents often enough. When they do go out to see them they always discover that it has been worth the effort because of new ideas which are born, because misunderstandings are put right, because of market information gleaned. (The best way to profit from a trip to an export agent is discussed later.)

A word of warning. "Regular contact" has been misinterpreted by some exporters. A Swedish textiles and fashion goods agent once opened his heart about his foreign principal. He had been visited very frequently, because in fact it was essential for the principal to go over at least twice a year to show the proposed styles for the coming season and to visit the main wholesalers to discuss designs. However, almost every time the principal sent over a different salesman, so that there was no chance for the agent to develop an understanding with one particular contact.

Continuity of personnel is something to aim for, because it takes time to build up an understanding when the two parties probably meet only two or three times a year for comparatively short periods.

Another complaint about visitors was voiced by the agent for a machine tool group. The parent company had a number of very self-contained manufacturing units, each with its own sales office specialising in a particular type of machine. There was a surface grinding division, an automatic lathe division, a horizontal boring division and so on. Each had the excellent system of paying six-monthly visits to every major overseas market, when they would accompany the agent on a tour of existing customers, showing the flag and discussing any technical problems.

However, as there were five divisions making these visits, with an average duration of one week, it meant that the agent was obliged to devote ten weeks a year to these tours, sometimes visiting the same clients with different sales engineers if the clients had bought more than one type of machine. In addition there was the work involved in correspondence in order to arrange each itinerary. For a long time the problem was that none of the executives who came over had any overall authority to take action on the agent's complaints. Each was only concerned with his own small unit.

This sort of problem can be solved or avoided by personal contact in the other direction—bringing the agent over to the principal's head office to meet the top men. This can serve a number of purposes. The agent is able to meet a bigger circle of the company's personnel, becoming acquainted with executives in service departments such as accounts, shipping, design, production, all activities which directly influence his market.

The agent's visit can be combined with further training, either through accompanying home salesmen on calls to important clients, or by attending a course of technical instruction for the servicing or installation of equipment, or by a visit to the firm's advertising agents or printers to learn about promotional developments.

Some agents arrange a visit to head office to coincide with the negotiation of an important contract, bringing the potential customer with them. The customer, too, can be impressed simultaneously with a tour of the factory or a tour of major installations of the principal's equipment in the home market.

Alternatively, an agent's visit can be made to coincide with the visit of agents from other territories so that a general export conference can be held. This gives everyone the chance to exchange good ideas, solve common problems and organise possible multilateral business introductions for the future. Several firms see to it that some form of presentation is made to one of the agents for his record turnover or rate of increase in sales. It shows the lucky agent and the others that the principals are aware of their efforts and appreciative of special efforts.

Again, the conference has a double impact because it impresses on the principal's own staff that these agents are real people whose cries for help, quotations, or information should be attended to promptly.

Conferences, however, should not be just an excuse for a get-together. It is advisable to have an objective which is clear to all participants. It then shows that the operation is business-like and makes the agents feel that the time spent was worthwhile. Remember, whilst they are away from their markets they are not earning commission, so indirectly they could be paying a high price for the privilege to attend the conference even if the principal meets all expenses. The occasion should coincide with the launching of something new and important, preferably something which is likely to increase their profits in the future. It might be a new model or a new marketing technique.

MAKING THE MOST OF A FOREIGN TOUR

Although it has been stated that it is desirable to maintain personal contact with regular visits to agents in export markets, it is obviously not enough simply to show one's face for its own sake no matter how fine a face one might have. Nor is it enough to visit an agent like an inspecting officer, asking if everything is all right and seeing that all the sales literature has been properly filed and the orders neatly folded on the desk. Neither is it advisable to creep up on an agent to catch him in the act of sitting back with a cigar when he should be on the road hitting clients over the head.

As the foreign tour usually takes place only two or three times a year to any one agent and as it is the major occasion for principal and agent to reinforce their partnership, it might as well be properly handled so that the right balance is achieved: a bit of all three of the aforementioned results. The sales tour allows the principal to show the flag, to pass an eye over the way things are going, to solve problems and to stimulate and encourage the agent to bigger and better sales efforts. Basically, in an export market the agent sells to the customers and the principal sells to the agent. He, above all, needs to be convinced of the worth of the product and the organisation behind it.

The following procedure has been found to work admirably by a large number of exporters in many different fields, consumer and industrial. First, the principal gives two or three months advance notice to the agent of the exact dates of his next visit. He asks him to confirm that the times will be convenient. The exporter does not want to plan his trip to coincide with a local national holiday or week of fasting or to clash with the agent's honeymoon.

Then the agent is asked to prepare a list of possible calls that they could make together during the visit, some to strengthen contacts with established customers, some to break new ground with potential customers. The agent is usually pleased to be able to bring a big gun from head office to bear on someone who has been putting up unnecessary sales resistance. The principal also sends the names and addresses of some contacts and inquiries of his own. The agent is told that the final selection will be made on the spot when they have had a chance to discuss the pros and cons.

In this way the agent is obliged to do a fair amount of fieldwork with clients before the manufacturer arrives. It avoids the temptation to just show off a small handpicked reliable group of old pal customers. Sales pressure is exerted in advance of the tour—all to the benefit of the principal. After all, when one principal is not putting on pressure, another one is. It is a good thing to have at least as long a turn as possible.

It is true that the exporter is competing for the selling time of his agent against the pressures from other principals he represents. On the other hand it must also be borne in mind that the agent must serve more than one master. He cannot be monopolised, especially as his business could probably not prosper on just your commission alone. (If it could, it is possibly wrong to be using an agent instead of a salaried employee.)

Therefore, when making sales calls with the agent, it is often a courteous and appreciated gesture to allow the agent and the client time to discuss other matters of business to do with other ranges of products once your side has been adequately covered. This will prevent the agent from feeling rather uneasy at the time he is giving exclusively to one account when other manufacturers will be breathing down his neck after your departure.

Every sales tour to a foreign market must have clearly defined objectives. The best thing is to have these written down on an agenda, so that there is no chance for vagueness to cloud the issues. One has to conceive of writing a report after the trip, setting down the concrete results achieved. These might be:

1   To persuade the agent to take on a new line
2   To change the commission structure
3   To persuade a distributor to hold bigger stocks
4   To convince the agent of the need to exhibit at a show
5   To educate his salesmen into selling bigger units
6   To institute a new system of sales reports
7   To agree a bigger target for the following year

These objectives must be attained in practice and not only in theory. Let the agent have a duplicate of any report submitted to the board of directors back home, confirming the agreement on specific points. Then the agent can be reminded if he does not move over to the new system worked out. He will also be pleased to note that something concrete was achieved as a result of the visit.

One of the advantages of having an agent in a foreign market is the local man's knowledge of market conditions. This must not, however, be taken entirely for granted. A too gullible visiting exporter tempts the agent to make up for laxity with a fertile imagination. Some very experienced exporters make use of a system of country and client index cards. The relevant ones are put into their briefcases before a journey to a foreign market. The country card will include:

1   Population figures
2   Market trend statistics
3   Degree of saturation by competitors
4   Number of potential outlets
5   Rate of progress in market
6   Orders on hand
7   Comparable situation the previous year, etc

This will show the agent that when this principal, at least, says he is coming on a visit, then socks have to be pulled up and spade-work has to be done. These statistics, by the way, should have been produced initially before an agent was appointed, at the time the market itself was chosen. They should then have been kept up to date. The client card will include:

1   Name, address, telephone, telex
2   Name of main contact
3   Name of man who really specifies, if different

4   Method of payment
5   Special packaging requirements
6   Any special mannerisms in ordering
7   History of orders to date
8   Personal notes (hobbies, birthday, etc)
9   OBJECTIVE (what is to be achieved by a call?—clinch an order, explain an error, increase size of deliveries, ask for introductions, etc)

These cards can be updated as the result of the tour. They are invaluable if ever there is a change of agent, for it must always be borne in mind that the customers are really the principal's, not the agents. The exporter's interest is to develop the market for his own goods. The agent must be seen as the means of doing that. He might do the selling and make the regular calls, but the market is more permanent than the agent, except where these precautions have not been taken.

MOTIVATING THE AGENT

The whole of this book should really come under this heading. In this section, however, we can include some specific schemes to create incentive.

Sole Rights. If an agent has not got sole rights in his territory then, as an experienced trader said, he will not "market" the goods, he will merely "flog" them. But the sole rights need not be handed over as a matter of course. One very successful exporter of technical equipment makes his agents compete to maintain sole rights. He divides a large country into smaller, compact sales territories, appointing an agent in each. There is an agreed six-monthly target according to the territory and the stage of marketing. If the target is not achieved, then the agent can be deprived of his exclusive rights. If the exporter is confident of his product, then this approach can work.

Commission Structure. The most common arrangement is straight commission on sales at an agreed standard percentage. This is usually the least effective system.

It is far better to work out a scheme where the commission

not only serves as remuneration for the agent but at the same time acts as a guide and an incentive.

For example, new markets or new products should be developed by offering higher commission for a given introductory period. This can be varied by offering commission on the standard price of a product even though prices are reduced during a launch. This allows the agent to earn proportionately more and ensures a fair share of the selling time being devoted to an otherwise less profitable account from the agent's point of view.

In an established territory a marketing policy should define whether increased volume is the main aim (due perhaps to a growing demand for that type of product), or an accelerating increase in sales (when saturation point is not yet in sight), or a bigger share of a static demand (at the expense of competitors' figures). Bonuses or variable commission rates could be tied to targets based on whichever objective is aimed at. Without this approach an agent and his principal might be delighted to jog along with a bigger turnover, when in fact they were losing out on their share of the expanding market.

Alternatively, the commission structure could be aimed at the *means* of achieving these targets. For example, some research might show that the most effective way to increase the *profitability* of the market would be to persuade existing customers to buy in larger quantities. This might result not only in a bigger volume of turnover but also in a reduction of unit overheads, cutting down the percentage cost of packaging, accounting, invoicing, and shipping. Commission could, in this instance, be based on the normal for volume plus an extra for every customer's order which is bigger than his previous one.

Another example is to offer a bonus commission for every order from a new client. Sometimes, where design considerations are important because orders are made to specification, special commission rates can be offered for repeat orders which are simpler to handle than new business.

Commission is too valuable a tool to be used unimaginatively as a blunt percentage on general turnover. That practice tends to discourage imagination on the part of the agent who may be unaware of the type of order which best suits the firm.

Agency Contract. Although the legal agreement between

principal and agent is designed to govern any possible disputes and to protect each party's interests in law, it can also serve as a plan of action. Clauses can set targets, detail the financial incentives outlined above and define penalties (loss of exclusive rights, termination of agreement) if targets are not achieved. The agreement can be a yardstick against which to measure promises. Naturally, prior research into market potential is essential before this sort of planning can be tackled.

An agreement should be looked upon also as a means of obliging the agent to make the most of the market. It is feasible, if the product is a good one, that once a certain comfortable turnover has been established, the agent will relax his efforts and spend his time counting his commission in his back room. An agreement can be phrased to make it compulsory for him to bring in a given amount of new business, otherwise the contract is to be terminated. The principal can stick to these terms so long as his assessment of the territory indicates that it is a long way from saturation.

Competition on International Scale. It was mentioned in the previous section on conferences that recognition can be given publicly to any special achievement, so that the agents in other countries are aware of this. One agent was invited back to his principal's country at the time of a national exhibition and publicly presented at a reception on the group stand with a plaque commemorating the year's best progress in any export market. A photograph appeared in the local press and also in the press of the area where the agent operated. He was justifiably proud of this recognition and, of course, he felt encouraged, almost bounden, to keep up the good work. Meanwhile other agents were reviewing their methods with a view to winning the award next time round.

ASSESSING AN AGENT'S PERFORMANCE

Many manufacturers, when reappraising their progress, or lack of it, in overseas markets, come face to face with the fact that they know very little about some of their agents. Usually they know least about those in the most unsuccessful areas.

On hundreds of occasions, if not thousands, agents have been sacked when the fault has lain with the product, the competition or with the principal himself.

As it is essential to have a clear picture of the agent's performance and of the backing he has received from his principal before a proper evaluation can be made of his worth, the following two procedures are recommended. They are known to have worked successfully on behalf of exporters who have made striking progress.

1 Comparative Performance Charts. These could serve a dual purpose. They can record export progress for the company's benefit and at the same time permit each foreign agent to compare his own results, on a properly adjusted basis, with the general trend. Each would feel encouraged by his placing or spurred to improve to avoid losing the account. If an agent has shown himself ineffective, when the time comes to sack him, there would be no question that he had been warned sufficiently well in advance by the regular provision of these statistics. The charts should cover the following data:

1   Sales for each territory
2   Sales adjusted according to size of territory
3   Share of market *vis-à-vis* main competitors
4   Rate of increase in sales
5   Average size of order per customer
6   Analysis by outlet
7   Analysis by type of product (if more than one)

The production of this data will keep the exporting firm well aware of the performance of all its agents. Weak ones will soon become apparent, with some guide to reasons for their weakness. At the same time, any general trend of international sales will strike the executive controlling exports early enough for him to consider what action needs to be taken.

If there is a general drop in the average size of orders, or if ground is being lost in more than one market to the same competition, he will know it is not simply the agent's fault, but will look further for the reason.

This system of standardised, regular charting protects the interests of the agent and the principal.

2 An Independent Questionnaire—about the principal!
Having discovered from the charts that an agent is faltering, rather than immediately indulging in the high cost and bother of sacking the old one and finding and training a new one, it is advisable to check that one's own firm has been providing the right whole-hearted support at all levels—from top management to the export salesmen and clerical staff.

A very novel but extremely effective way of doing this is to ask an outside organisation to interview the agent with the following type of questionnaire, forming, perhaps, part of a more comprehensive evaluation of the agent's whole organisation and sales approach. The questionnaire will discover *what the agent's evaluation is of the principal.*

1   What percentage of your total revenue is earned as a result of your representation of this particular principal?
2   How does the time that you allocate to this account relate to your earnings from it?
3   How do you think the principal relates the time you spend on his behalf to the commission you earn?
4   Is your principal aware of these facts? If not, why not?
5   Assuming that the market for the product had been researched and agreed at your appointment, and that practical experience now confirms the potential, then what is your view of your principal under the following heading:

(*a*) Is he adhering to the terms of the agreement?
(*b*) How often do you meet (i) the chairman or president —personally? (ii) other senior executives? (iii) his local factory rep?
(*c*) How does he normally communicate—letter, telex, telephone? Is this method of communication satisfactory? Is it rapid enough?

6   Have you complete confidence in the product you are selling?
7   Do you receive satisfactory sales support as follows:

(*a*) Technical sales visits—is the technical sales staff

available when really needed, provided you give adequate notice?

(b) Service facilities—does the principal offer a spares and maintenance service as good as that of your main competitors?

(c) Sales literature—is it adequate? If not, how can it be improved? Is the language correct? Is the data in it sufficient? Is it readily understandable from the point of view of language, terminology, and approach? Does it stress the advantages or merely explain the product?

(d) Exhibitions—is proper advantage taken of the opportunities to exhibit? Is there a budget to allow you to keep up with the competition?

(e) Demonstrations—can they be organised when you stress that they are necessary? Does the principal send senior management executives or only the machine demonstrator? Does he send no one, leaving it to you?

(f) Are sufficiently senior executives sent out when you request their presence? Do they readily visit you to discuss the enlargement of the market or the development of a new market?

(g) If executives call, are they adequately informed on your market and its history? Have they been delegated enough authority to make decisions? Have they enough time available to settle the important matters you wish discussed?

(h) When a visiting executive returns to head office, does he see that promises are kept and that decisions are carried through effectively?

The Scottish poet Robert Burns said:

> *O wad some Pow'r the giftie gie us*
> *To see oursels as ithers see us!*

It may not be a gift, but in the export business it is certainly possible to purchase this asset by asking a consultant to discover what image the agent has of the manufacturer. The description is sometimes very different from the picture the manufacturer has of himself. It can be particularly illuminating if this procedure is carried out with more than one agent, to see if the impressions tally. It can be a short-cut to reshaping an export effort which will really bring results, and maybe save innocent agents from the high jump.

If all this checking, selecting, charting, training, motivating, and interrogating still produces an agent who does not operate satisfactorily, the sooner he is relieved of his duties the better. Wrong selections can be made. It is not a failure to admit it. It *is* a serious failure to do nothing about it.

The next chapter will act as a guide to the requirements of the agent. If these are met and still the promise is unfulfilled, the relationship will have to be terminated. But, before doing that, it is wise to have a look at the clauses of the contract and the special legislation which might prevail in the country concerned (see Chapters 7 and 8).

CHAPTER 6

What the Agent Expects From You

After a war it often happens that the victor forces very stringent treaty terms on the vanquished. These terms often then lead to serious friction as soon as the weaker party has gained sufficient strength to argue again.

This is a mistake which exporters must avoid. If they find a willing agent, they must not immediately attempt to negotiate terms which the agent will eventually have to fight against when he has established the market.

Naturally this book, being aimed primarily to help manufacturers achieve the best results, has tended so far to stress the means of safeguarding the interests of the manufacturer *vis-à-vis* the agent. But one of the best methods of producing harmonious relations is for the manufacturer to appreciate at the earliest stage what conditions will make the agent most content, most co-operative and, in the long run, most effective on his behalf.

The exporter or manufacturer must be clear about his own objectives when appointing an agent and must ensure that certain basic requirements of his own are met. But he must be equally clear what the agent expects and he must be prepared to meet the agent on points basic to the other party's welfare.

CHECKING BACK ON THE PRINCIPAL

In many respects the agent's requirements are similar to those of his principal. He needs to be sure that he will be working on behalf of a company which is solvent and stable. An agent is supplying his services in advance of payment. He does not want to discover after months of investment of time and money that his commission cannot be honoured because the principal has gone out of business. He is likely therefore to look into a prospective employer's credit worthiness. If there is any reason to suspect that a report might not be entirely favourable, it is a good idea to explain this in advance, as diplomatically and honestly as possible. Firms, for example, can have gone through a bad patch, can have been refinanced or have had a change of management to overcome flaws. The agent ought to be told and given a chance to assess the prospects of improvement. If he is a good agent, the kind you want, he will check up and it may be through sources less up to date than yourself.

In the same way an agent will almost certainly wish to refer to your previous agent in the market if you are making a change. It would be impossible to prevent this, so give full and factual reasons for the change, with due acknowledgement of any points on which your firm has been at fault. An admission of these with an account of the steps already taken or planned to rectify mistakes will do more to satisfy the new man than any attempt to gloss over them.

Not only is it a good idea to talk about the previous agency experience, in some countries it is essential in law. There are regulations which stipulate that no agent can take on a new principal unless the previous agent in that market has voluntarily relinquished the agreement or been adequately compensated. The new man must therefore check with the previous one before signing a contract.

It is obviously to the exporter's advantage if the new agent is able to contact the previous agent on friendly terms, taking over relevant documents, some know-how and any existing service contracts with customers. Changing agents in a market can be a ticklish procedure and the new one will be as keen as the exporter to contribute as much as possible to a smooth handing over. He will expect complete frankness from the exporter. Sooner or later, from the old agent or from the existing customers, he will learn the worst anyway!

ANALYSIS OF THE PRINCIPAL

Short of completely secret information (and this is usually a very small area indeed when one is objective about it), the fullest details must be given to the agent about a company's capital rating, turn-over, rate of growth, plans for the future, number of people employed, number and size of factories, range of products, export performance, and general company policy and outlook. The agent needs to know for himself and he will also be asked one or other of these questions by clients as he markets your products.

Ideally, the agent should be involved in the drawing up of a forward financial plan for the penetration of his market in terms of turnover and his planned income arising from this. He requires sufficient information on the company's plans for the territory so that he can genuinely feel personally involved in bringing about the success of the marketing plan.

The agent should also be told as much as possible about the organisation of exports at head office, with a clear outline of the chain of command there. If possible he should be given a direct contact with some executive who is always on hand at the export office to provide immediate servicing of problems. Too frequently the liaison is exclusively through an export salesman or sales manager who is so often away on trips that the unfortunate agents can only rarely obtain quick answers to their questions.

ANALYSIS OF THE PRODUCT

When negotiating with a new agent, the manufacturer has to be prepared with answers to a large number of questions on the nature of the product and the production facilities behind the product.

The negotiator must be clear in his own mind on the applications of the product, the type of outlets likely to offer the most business potential and the terms of payment which can be offered.

The agent has to know at the outset how quotations are pre-pared—f.o.b., c.i.f., or c.i.f. duty paid—and which currency will be quoted. Invoicing procedure must be carefully explained, with examples of invoices where possible. In the early days he will probably receive some urgent requests for the explanation of an invoice from new clients.

Are discounts available for quick settlement of accounts, and is his commission based on the original invoiced amount or the net paid? How are the goods packed for dispatch to the client? These details can all play a part in the agent's assessment of his chances on the market and, if he takes on the agency, in his approach to selling.

There are many aspects of production and delivery which must be known so that he can gear his tempo of selling to the principal's facilities. For example, are there likely to be any seasonal fluctuations of either demand, supply, or price? It might well be that the exporter is looking for export markets to take up the slack at particular seasons of the year. If so, then this must be explicitly stated and not left to the agent to discover to his cost later. Frankness is always recommended so that the agent can feel integrated into the exporter's sales efforts. He must know the weaknesses as well as the strengths of the product and the firm. It is essential for him to be informed about stocks. If there is an accumulation due to poor sales in other markets, this could be his opportunity to sell hard and obtain orders on the promise of quick deliveries. On the other hand, if manufacturing facilities cannot meet present orders he must be aware that his selling ought to be played on a more long-term note. He might welcome the opportunity of selling-in your products gently at the beginning whilst concentrating mainly on other principals' products which will gain him his immediate revenue.

The exporter should inform the agent about the size of his home market and its rate of expansion or otherwise. He should give details about the size of the export business and its rate of growth, indicating which areas are already covered and which areas are being investigated. Export marketing is best seen as multilateral, with a co-ordinated global approach. There can often be useful interaction amongst agents in different foreign markets, exchanging leads, arranging for clients to visit installations nearer than those in the home market, introducing goods to a client via his associated company which might already be a client in another territory.

The agent expects this type of information, for the more help he gets in selling, from any source, the happier he is about his own prospects and working for you.

Naturally, one of the main points on which the new agent wants to be crystal clear is the advantage which your product can be said to have over competitors in his market. The exporter must therefore be able to give an analysis of the characteristics of the different rival products in the field, enabling the agent to assess his chances of introducing the goods in the face of existing competition. It is possible he might latch on to other aspects as main selling points, other than those stressed in the home market. For example, quick delivery might be the best sales weapon because of local capacity shortages, but he can only judge when all the details have been made clear.

MARKET RESEARCH

In attempting to put over these facts and figures, it may become evident that neither the agent nor the manufacturer has enough statistics or market information for a clear-cut campaign to be devised. The earlier this is realised the better, for it will bring up the question of the need for market research. This can be a fairly costly item. Who will pay for it?

The agent will wish to know to what extent his principal would be willing to have the necessary research carried out for him, or to what extent he will contribute to its cost. Agreement must be reached on the objectives of any research so that both parties are eventually happy that the money invested has achieved what they wanted. These objectives must be committed to paper, for large numbers of good business relationships have foundered on the arguments, after an expensive research programme has been carried out, about what they had really been trying to find out in the first place.

The market research can of course cover many facets of an operation to launch products on to a new market. It can cover the qualities, prices, and market shares of competitive products. It can investigate the money being spent by competitors to promote their products, and the media used; it can attempt to evaluate the future growth of the market; it can define the biggest outlets and the best distribution channels for different products. It can assess customer motivation and reaction to different aspects of a product to see which selling point is most effective.

Not all these aspects need to be researched for every product. That is why the agent must be aware of what data are already known and available to him, what other data are essential, and how much he might have to afford personally to fill in the gaps.

THE CONTRACT—FROM THE AGENT'S POINT OF VIEW

It has to be remembered that an agent is likely to feel insecure if too many agreements are verbal and insufficiently documented in the contract. Early negotiations can run smoothly with a great sense of understanding and bonhomie between the people taking part. However, the agent is generally the smaller of the two contracting parties and may feel more vulnerable to changes in the principal company's staff and to misunderstandings in the future.

Contracts are of course hardly needed when things go well. Sales are made, delivery times met, customers pay their bills, the commission is paid promptly into the agent's bank and the product is praised by all who use it or consume it.

But each one of these activities can cause serious problems if anything goes wrong. The objective to aim for is a quick solution to a problem with everyone knowing exactly what his responsibility is. Moments of stress are the worst possible times for an argument about terms agreed and yet they are the most likely times.

Contract problems can arise from omissions or from over-zealousness of the stronger party to cherish his own interests so that the terms begin to pinch at the agent's toes as time goes on. As mentioned earlier, the contract should suit both sides and not act as a means of obtaining a stranglehold.

Contract clauses, on commission, credit risk, conditions of sale, and so on, warrant more lengthy treatment elsewhere in this book. (See Chapter 7 and Appendix 6.) Some of the major interests which the agent likes to see defined in his contract, points which tend to be overlooked by the principal, are described below.

Territory Definition. The agent does not want to be allocated an area in which he does not do much travelling for his other accounts. It is economic for both sides when the agent is covering a specific territory thoroughly in frequency and depth for all his principals.

At the same time he does not want to have his own strong area divided between himself and another agent with the result that he is calling on clients with one product whilst they are being serviced for another of his products by someone else.

Product Range. It must be clear which of the principal's products the agent is really taking on. He may not wish to be judged as a poor performer because he is not selling certain products of the principal's range which do not fit in with the general run of calls he makes.

Similarly, he cannot just be expected automatically to become agent for each new product launched in the future by the principal. There should be a new agreement for additions to his range and this may well involve a new commission structure. However, at the same time, if the agent is doing a good job for the principal he would like to have the option of taking on any new products before they are offered elsewhere.

Outlet Definition. If, for example, an agent has excellent regular contacts with retail shops, selling some type of lighting or display fittings, he will not expect to be resented later because he has not sold very much to factories. A product could conceivably overlap across the calls an agent makes and a potential market he never touches.

The principal has to decide whether to have two agents for different outlets (say, retail and industrial); or whether to appoint one agent for the main outlet and let the other slide; or whether to seek another type of agent who can cover both markets simultaneously.

Non-Profit-Making Activities. An agent expects to give a good service to promote the products and the prestige of his principal, but he cannot afford to devote too much of his time to activities outside the specific realm of selling for a commission.

These activities might be after-sales servicing, warehousing, storing of stocks, market analysis, over-lengthy reports and forecasts or calls on "house accounts" which the exporter has reserved for himself. Training sessions are another no-revenue activity which some principals demand too selfishly. The principal must bear constantly in mind that the agent works on commission and must concentrate on selling in order to keep up his rate of remuneration. That is not to say that these other activities must be neglected. If they are essential then they must be costed separately and agreements made to cover them.

If a product is best sold from large stocks, if the product

is technical and requires servicing, if the agent and his salesmen must be trained at regular intervals in either technical matters or in methods of selling, then it must be agreed at the outset and in writing to what extent the agent will be able to claim additional remuneration for time spent and for extra accommodation he might have to rent.

In the early stages of developing a new market these matters might be trivial, but if the market grows to everyone's expectations they can become a big burden and a source of discontent to undo the previous good work.

Expenses. Most agents working on commission will pay their own normal sales expenses of travel, correspondence, and telephones, etc. There are, however, other areas of expense which ought to be defined so that responsibility can be agreed in writing. These include the cost of inviting potential clients back to the factory, the insurance of goods being carried as samples by the agent, the frequency of visits to head office by the agent. Perhaps he will be willing to pay his own way once or twice a year, but if there is a sales conference or a special new product launching or a meeting on participation at an exhibition, then probably his travel expenses should be met by the principal.

It ought to be agreed in advance, with the contract defining the agent's responsibilities, unforeseen occasions being negotiated as they arise.

Duration of Contract. The agent requires security. He can only willingly invest his maximum effort if he is secure in the knowledge that his early returns, although small, will be compensated for later when the product is established. This is, of course, exactly the attitude which will bring most benefit to the manufacturer. To achieve it the agent requires a contract which guarantees long-term benefits. Perhaps it is better for both sides to have a provisional clause at first, in case either party feels a mistake has been made after a few months—there may be a trial period of six months.

Subsequently the agent will want a guarantee of at least a year, if not two years, with six months' prior notice if the agreement is not to be renewed.

PROMPT SERVICE

Finally, and this is something which cannot really be spelt out in a contract, the agent demands the fullest co-operation from the principal's company, especially in the early stages. His letters must be answered as a priority, his commission must be paid promptly and his invited guests received well at head office.

So many agents have said that they feel they are treated as "funny foreigners" when they request something. This can happen if the export office staff has not been made sufficiently aware of the problems an agent is facing or of the special requirements of his market.

Another major complaint from agents is that their main contact at head office is always changing. One agent told how he had been visited during a period of sixteen years by almost thirty different salesmen from head office. Each time he had the task of introducing them to the major clients in his market. This lack of continuity broke his spirit, for there was no growth of a personal relationship and, of course, very few promises were ever kept when the salesman returned home.

Apparently (and this is surprisingly common) some manufacturers can regard an export tour as a "perk." Salesmen who have done well on the home market are given a trip abroad as a sort of reward. The tendency even is to send them to the market with the best agent so that they can be suitably impressed.

Nice for the salesman, but disastrous for the agent whose market is thus regarded as a playground.

CHAPTER 7

The Contract

There are not only two parties to the contract, but there are also two sides to it—the business side and the legal side.

The principal and the agent should define in their own minds and then in writing, in advance of the actual contract, the objectives they wish to achieve. These preliminary documents might almost be a plan of action as well as a list of minimum requirements.

When the two parties are agreed in essence on what they will give and take to satisfy each other's demands, then expert legal advice should be called upon to ensure three things:

1   That the phraseology and scope of the clauses do in fact achieve what they are intended to achieve without possibility of misinterpretation

2   That the contract meets the requirements of law judged from the point of view of both legal systems which might become involved (home and foreign)

3   That the implications of the contract do not, for example, unwittingly bring either party unnecessarily into disadvantage within the tax laws of either country

The old expression "prepare for the worst and hope for the best" should be borne in mind when working out an agency agreement, because it is usually only in the worst circumstances that they are referred to. They only come into play when a normal working relationship has broken down, when a dispute cannot be resolved by mutual understanding. If outside arbitration or even litigation has to be resorted to, then the more watertight the contract the better, to safeguard legitimate interests.

What is more, it is a good idea to have a note in a diary, well in advance, to update the terms of a contract periodically. It usually gives cause for a good laugh when an old dusty contract is looked at eight or ten years after it has been signed, for many of the terms would make nonsense of existing business arrangements between the two parties. If the contract is only come across accidentally or looked up for a laugh, fair enough, but if the ancient document is hurriedly sought because of impending litigation, the laughter might sound very hollow.

Both parties should be grateful for a comprehensive contract as the whole purpose is to give security to their operations.

Types of agreement will differ according to whether the agent is acting solely in a selling capacity, or purchasing the goods on his own account for resale, or stocking goods on consignment and selling them on commission. In each case there are entirely different interests to safeguard. The commission agent is not buying anything, not being employed, not taking responsibility for goods or credit. The relationship is a curious one and more difficult to define.

If the agent is a stockist or distributor buying the products himself, then the agreement is more a contract of sale with certain conditions in return for special terms, such as exclusive right to buy in the area. One of the conditions of sale might be that the agent will not purchase competitive products.

Where stocks are delivered on consignment, the contract has to make clear, for example, that they remain the property of the principal. It is rather a sticky situation if an agent goes bankrupt and his creditors claim all the goods in his warehouse, when these belong to the foreign manufacturer!

It is not very difficult to imagine a whole string of queries which might arise in the course of an agency-principal relationship and which might require recourse to the contract to settle. Here are some examples:

1   Was the agreement made with the individual or his firm?
2   Can the agent assign the agreement to his successor or sell it as part of the goodwill of his business, leaving the principal represented by someone else?
3   Where the document is in two languages, which is the original with authority in case of a difference of interpretation?

4   If the principal brings out a new, related product, is he at liberty to appoint another agent to handle it?

5   Or is the agent appointed for the whole of the principal's programme, representing the firm rather than the products?

6   What is the definition of the origin of an order? If it is placed by, say, a buying house in Paris, for delivery to Chad, does the African or French agent qualify for commission?

7   Is the principal at liberty to negotiate special terms inside his domestic market with visiting buyers from the agent's territory who refuse to purchase through a local agent? (See instance on page 33)

8   Is commission on the gross sum invoiced or only on the net value of goods? (Less freight charges insurance, etc)

9   What is the agreed method of quoting?

10   Who is responsible for payment of inland carriage?

11   Who is responsible for insurance cover of stocks held on consignment? (No use arguing after the fire!)

12   If urgent cables are required for a contract, which party defrays the cost?

13   If the principal is unable to fulfil a sales contract or cannot accept an order because of production or delivery problems, can the agent buy from an alternative source to satisfy a customer?

14   What notice is required to terminate an agreement and what are the compensation terms for premature termination?

15   Is the agreement for a fixed period and what is the procedure for renewal?

Specific clauses to cover any of these questions, and many others like them, should be included in a comprehensive agreement, just in case.

The whole matter of contracts is so important and causes so many difficulties, that the International Chamber of Commerce, whose head office is in Paris, set up a commission on international commercial practice. This drafted a "Guide for the Drawing Up of Contracts between Parties Residing in Different Countries" which was approved by the ICC Council. The Chamber was kind enough to give permission for the whole of their recommendations to be published in this book. They appear in Appendix 6.

For the benefit of all executives involved in international trade, the Institute of Export in London has produced specimens of three types of agency agreements. These represent possible types of contracts for:

1   Exclusive and sole agents representing manufacturers overseas
2   Merchant firm having its own branches or head office in overseas territory, buying as principals and paying cash for stock, at time of shipment
3   Agents appointed overseas to whom stocks are shipped on consignment account

The London Chamber of Commerce also makes available a "Specimen Agreement for Agent in Overseas Market."

The Institute of Export and the London Chamber of Commerce have been good enough to grant permission to have these specimen contracts reproduced in this book. They are intended only as examples of the way agreements can be drawn up and it is emphasised that manufacturers should always ensure that an agreement is formulated to suit the particular needs of his circumstances. As the Institute points out, "in cases of doubt, or where the agreement covers transactions involving large sums of money, credit facilities and other arrangements, the services of qualified solicitors are indispensable."

The Institute suggests, however, that "in many instances the agreement is either with agents who through time have given their principals some measure of confidence as to their competence and integrity, or with agents operating on a scale which barely justifies the engagement of solicitors for the drafting of separate agreements. The three specimen agency agreements are suitable for dealings of this nature.

"They have been drafted by independent lawyers with intimate knowledge of export legislation, and approved by the Legal Committee of the Institute of Export. The agreements have proved their worth on innumerable occasions and many exporters' current agency agreements are known to be based on them."

The specimen agreements are reproduced in Appendix 7.

To keep a balance, it might now be as well to give another point of view. The *British Agents Review* in January 1967 and again in January 1968 published a warning to its readers on the "Fallacies and Dangers of Standard Agreements."

They suggest that "the use of any standard agreement is dangerous to the agent in that it limits the protection afforded to the agent. The limitations lie in the number of clauses it contains, the scope of the wording used and, not the least important, the amount of space left on any printed agreement for inserting agreed conditions! . . . Basically, an agent needs to compile his own check list of all the problems that are likely to arise with any one agency. . . . Having prepared his checklist, the agent should then discuss and clarify each clause in it with the principal concerned. When agreement (or compromise) is reached, the agreement itself should be drafted by a solicitor."

That is the view taken by an organisation concerned with the interests of agents. It is probably safest for the principal to use a similar approach. As suggested at the opening of this chapter, the fair and sure way is for both sides to work out their own objectives and agree a contract, vetted by legal experts, which fits exactly their joint requirements. The very act of working over the agreement together is combined thinking on marketing and sales organisation which can result in many side benefits. Often a vague understanding produces a vague approach to the market.

One last, yet important, aspect of contracts to bear in mind is the confirmation that the agent is competent to enter into an agreement. In many countries, for example in the Middle East (Libya, Iraq, United Arab Republic), in the Far East (Taiwan), in Latin America (Costa Rica, Dominican Republic), agents must be local citizens, registered for trading with some commercial authority, solvent, etc. In New Zealand the import licensing system might prevent an agent from bringing your goods into the country. In Eastern Europe only state foreign trading companies or state agency companies are permitted to act as agents.

It is unfortunately necessary to glance through the following two chapters to gain a general idea of the factors which might have to be taken into account. The consoling thought is that when the right contract has been signed with the right agent in the right market then that part of the world is tied up effectively for many years to come.

CHAPTER 8

Special Laws on Agency Relationships in Different Parts of the World

People who have gone on dangerous assignments wearing bullet-proof vests have sometimes succumbed to poisoning. It is advisable to know as much as possible about the other party's aims and intentions and methods of operation before the actual confrontation.

Agency agreements are not such life and death matters, thank goodness, but it pays to be briefed in advance on the general situation of a country and the objectives dear to its heart. Normally the tendency is to think only in terms of experience at home, whereas the other party in a foreign market has had such different problems to face that he is conditioned to view things in quite another light.

LEGISLATIVE GROUNDS

In the majority of countries the normal law of contract applies to agency agreements, with their own written clauses or standard business procedure governing any possible future disputes. However, there are many important exceptions where governments have introduced legislation expressly to apply to relationships between agent and principal. These laws do not all stem from the same type of problem, but can result from any permutation of the following five legislative grounds:

1 Fair Play. Sad to relate, there have been examples, internationally, of unscrupulous agents and unscrupulous principals.

So often a relationship sours between two well-meaning parties and one takes advantage of a position of power over the other. Many countries have found it necessary to enact legislation to safeguard the injured parties by law. Countries such as Austria, Germany, Sweden, and Switzerland have issued detailed regulations indicating minimum requirements of fair agreements, paying particular attention to matters of compensation when agreements are prematurely terminated. It has been known for principals to cancel an agency agreement when a large amount of work has been done, just prior to the signing of a big order, leaving the agent with no commission to reward his efforts.

There have also been instances of principals allowing agents to spend time and money obtaining orders and then simply failing to deliver the goods (occasionally as a result of giving the home market priority during periods of scarcity) with the result that the agency loses his commission on an unfulfilled contract.

In other cases, agents have been badly off after losing the rights to a product and having signed an early agreement with a clause prohibiting them from handling a competitive product for many years after.

Switzerland even has a regulation obliging the principal to provide some compensation to an agent who is unable to continue his activities for a period due to his entry into the Swiss armed forces!

2 Preserving Foreign Exchange. Quite a number of governments have produced laws which regulate the payment of commission so that it remains in the country, saving on the outflow of currency. Generally this can be achieved by ensuring that the whole or a major part of an agency firm is in the hands of local nationals who are bound to declare all their foreign currency earnings, handing them over to the local banks.

3 Interests of State Purchasing. Many governments are reluctant to pay their own local tradesmen a commission on what the state purchases. They prefer to buy direct from the foreign supplier just that much more cheaply. Guinea, for example, lays down that no exclusive agency rights apply when the state or a public utility is the customer. In the communist countries, of course, and to a certain extent in Egypt, the agencies are themselves state owned.

4 Protection of Local Economy. There are many territories where local industry or agriculture are extremely dependent upon materials or equipment supplied from overseas through the intermediary of agents. They cannot afford to leave important sectors of the economy vulnerable to changes in business policy. For example, some provinces of Canada have laws making it obligatory for agents handling farm machinery to maintain stocks of spares for ten years after any machine goes out of production.

A number of territories protect their economies by making sure that agents are really capable of providing the proper service for handling their agency lines. Agents are obliged to register their activities, giving proof of their business experience and of their solvency. Even in countries where local citizens are generally the only people allowed to take on agencies, exceptions are made to allow foreigners to handle the business if no local nationals are sufficiently qualified or trained to carry out efficient maintenance or installations. Libya makes it obligatory in those instances for the foreign principal to train Libyan citizens to take over the agency within one year.

5 Development of Local Trade. A growing number of the underdeveloped nations are concerned at the possibility of too much of their international trade remaining in the hands of expatriates. Countries in Latin America, the Middle East and Far East frequently stipulate that only local citizens can act as agents for the sale and importation of foreign goods. In Costa Rica, for example, foreign principals are obliged to give power of attorney, drawn up according to Costa Rican law, to local agents, indicating exactly what authority has been vested with the agents. In Libya only local nationals can act as agents and no one person can have an interest in more than ten agencies, so that as more principals are attracted to selling into Libya, so more local people have an opportunity to share in the developing trade.

Where there is no special legislation and the normal law of contract applies, especially in most developed countries, it is worth while taking a look at the provisions of a draft text drawn up by the Swedish Agents Association and submitted to the Federation of Nordic Commercial Agents in 1962. Although there might be difference of interpretation or opinion on various clauses, it certainly can serve as a guide to what a fairly advanced body of agents regard as fair play, based on business practice.

SUMMARY OF LEGISLATION IN TWENTY COUNTRIES

The following pages can act as a rough guide to the legal implications which might arise in different parts of the world. It must be stressed that it is merely a lay summary of legislative points and is in no way a substitute for professional consultation.

Exporters must note also that regulations can change quickly and that countries can introduce legislation where none previously existed. The intention of this chapter is to show simply what *might* arise and to emphasise that legal advice, locally and at home, is advisable when important matters are at stake.

Austria. The Mercantile Agents Law states that "the rights and duties arising out of the relation between principal and agent are in the first instance governed by the terms of the contract which subsists between them and only those points which are not dealt with in this contract are determined by the provisions of the Mercantile Agents Law. However, certain provisions contained in this Law cannot be cancelled or varied by the terms of the agency agreement if such cancellation or variation would operate to the agent's disadvantage."

It is interesting to note that the conduct or situation of the two parties can produce an "implied agency" even if there has been no written or verbal appointment. If an agent is not authorised by the principal to conclude a contract and yet does so in his name, then the principal must repudiate it to the third party as soon as it comes to his notice, otherwise it will be deemed ratified officially.

If the purchaser of goods or equipment rejects them within a specified period on the grounds of faulty condition, *vis-à-vis* the agent, this is binding upon the principal.

The principal cannot set up a private limitation upon the agent's ostensible authority, for as far as third parties are concerned the ostensible authority is the sole test of the principal's liability.

To the advantage of the principal, the Law states that the agent must safeguard the interests of the principal and apply reasonable care and diligence. If a transaction involves the granting of credit facilities the agent is obliged to satisfy himself of the financial standing of the customer. However, the existence of a *del credere* agency is not presumed. Furthermore, the agent is not allowed to accept a commission or remuneration from the customer unless it is customary in a particular line of business. If it happens, the principal is entitled to demand the surrender of the unlawful commission and claim even greater damages if appropriate.

If there are no relevant clauses in the agency agreement, then the Law applies to commission in the following way:

The agent is entitled to commission on any transaction brought about by his direct intervention. If he is not directly involved, he is entitled to commission during his agency period on any transaction with customers originally introduced by him or allocated to him, or within a territory exclusively allocated to him.

The agent is also entitled to commission on a transaction which falls through as a result of the principal's unreasonable conduct. If the agent merely gives the name of a prospective customer, then he is not entitled to claim commission, unless this is allowed for in the agreement.

Adequate compensation can be claimed by the agent if the principal prevents his obtaining his commission contrary to the agreement or if the agent is unable to earn or continue earning his commission due to the handing over of sales to another organisation or due to the principal's disposing of the business.

If no provision is made by agreement on the extent of commission to be paid, then the agent can claim the normal rate for the line of business. If the principal grants a rebate after a transaction has been finalised, then the agent can claim full commission on the original price, unless this is normal procedure in the line of business.

Unless other terms are fixed by agreement, then payment of commission falls due when accounts are settled at the end of each quarter. However, the agent is fully entitled to claim advance payments in respect of commission earned by him corresponding with the amount of his out-of-pocket expenses. The agent is entitled to an extract from the principal's account dealing with the transactions in respect of which commission is due to him.

Claim to commission and reimbursement of cash expenses is statute-barred after the lapse of three years.

Concerning the termination of an agency agreement, the following points of the Law are of special interest:

If there has been no specific period fixed for the duration of the agency agreement, or if the agency agreement continues after the fixed date by tacit consent, then each party may terminate it by six weeks' notice, counted to the end of a calendar quarter. If there has been a contractual relationship for more than five years, then the period of notice is three months. By agreement the period of notice can be longer or shorter or even nil so long as the same terms apply to both parties. If an agreement is made for different lengths of notice for each side, then the longer period is applicable to both parties by law.

Special rules on period of notice apply to lines of business affected by definite seasons. Normally notice is not allowed during or just prior to a "season," and this legal provision cannot be cancelled or varied by agreement between the parties even if it would not operate to the disadvantage of the agent.

An agency agreement can only be terminated prematurely on important grounds. These include the situation in which the agent becomes incapable of discharging his duties; when the agent forfeits his principal's confidence by, say, misrepresentation on important questions; if the agent neglects his affairs during a considerable period, or violates essential clauses of an agreement; or the occasions when an agent goes bankrupt.

Similarly, the agent can terminate the agreement prematurely if he finds he becomes incapable of discharging his duties, or if the principal withholds commission due to him, or violates any essential clauses in the contract.

If one of the parties terminates the agreement prematurely, then the other is entitled to claim compensation for the loss sustained. If this happens before the agency has been held for fifteen years, and the principal or his successor continues to benefit from work carried out by the agent during the agency period, then adequate compensation can be claimed, not in excess of one year's average commission based on the previous three years' business, or the whole period if less than three years. Where an agency agreement has lasted more than three years, then the maximum compensation claimable is diminished by one-twelfth for every additional year, until the point when no compensation can be claimed after an agency has lasted for more than fifteen years.

If the agency agreement was fixed for a definite period, then the agent can claim compensation in respect of the loss sustained by him if the principal goes bankrupt.

No clause can be valid in an agreement if it aims to restrict the agent in his business after the termination of the agreement.

Belgium. Belgian law on the subject of termination of agency agreements has been drawn up with the intention of safeguarding the interests of sole agents and concessionnaires who might have worked hard to develop a market and then find themselves dismissed just when they would begin to benefit.

It is mainly concerned with agency agreements which do not contain clauses to define the exact duration of the agreement or which do not lay down strict procedure for the termination of the contract.

When the principal unilaterally terminates the relationshp without reasonable cause or when the agent is obliged to terminate the contract because of serious default on the part of the principal, then the agent can go to court to claim "appropriate and equitable" compensation. This compensation will take into account:

1 Any increase of business resulting from the agent's efforts which will benefit the principal after the end of the relationship
2 Any expenses incurred by the agent which will result in future profit for the principal
3 The costs to be borne by the agent in discharging any staff because of the ending of the relationship

Belgian law applies when the dispute is between a Belgian agent and a foreign principal.

Bulgaria. See Chapter 9.

Canada. For the purpose of commercial law, Canada has to be seen as a federal state with certain special legislation applying only to particular provinces.

Generally, English legal precedent can be taken as determining the implications of a contract, but in Quebec, English precedent is not an authority to be quoted in cases which do not depend upon doctrines derived from English law.

In *Saskatchewan, Manitoba,* and *Alberta* the normal law of contract applies also to agency agreements, with the exception of the marketing of agricultural and farm machinery. Special legislation has been enacted to protect the interests of farmers who are so dependent upon the equipment they purchase. It obliges dealers to provide adequate spares and service facilities for any agricultural machinery they supply for ten years after the equipment has gone out of production.

China. See Chapter 9.

Colombia. Certain decrees have been issued by the Colombian authorities to put agents on a controlled footing.

All agents must register with the Public Registry of Commerce. This can be done at the agent's local chamber of commerce. He will then be provided with a certificate which proves his official right to act on behalf of the principal named. A check is also made on the foreign principal, who must have his credentials authorised by the Colombian Consul in his own country.

The registry will state the capacity in which the agent is authorised to act, the defined areas where he is permitted to operate and the goods, equipment, or services he is authorised to handle. The registration will remain valid until it is officially revoked or amended, this being achieved by presenting the relevant documents to the local chamber of commerce after giving ninety days' notice to the agent of any change in the working agreement. This term of notice dates from the time of registration of the new document.

To avoid unnecessary legal actions, disputes between agent and principal can be put to the good offices of the Colombian Federation of Representative Agents or the relevant chamber of commerce.

Official registration is vital when tendering for governmental or semi-official purchasing, for the chamber of commerce certificate must be submitted to prove that the agent is authorised in the correct fashion.

Costa Rica. Costa Rica is a state which is rigid on the question of which people or firms are permitted to act as agents and representatives. It is as well to know the basic conditions so that the exporter can be sure at the outset that he is not wasting his time with unregistrable agents.

The Costa Rican Commercial Law applies to "Travelling Agents and Representatives of Foreign Firms," whether these are salaried employees of the principal or acting in their own name on behalf of principals.

The principal is obliged to provide power of attorney or a letter of authority to the agents authorising them to act on his behalf. Agents must be Costa Rican citizens or, if not, permanently established in the national territory. They must have had some reasonable experience of commercial practice for not less than three years and to be of recognised solvency and integrity. These qualifications have to be registered in the Mercantile Register and a licence to act as the representative of a foreign firm has to be granted by the Ministry of Economy and Finance.

Any contract finalised between a customer and an agent is binding and comes under the jurisdiction of local law.

The total amount of his commission can be claimed by the agent on any business contract which does not come to fruition due to the principal's negligence or default.

Power of attorney and other legal agreements which have to be registered in Costa Rica are only acceptable if drawn up according to Costa Rican law, irrespective of the requirements of the foreign principal's own home law. It is usually safest, when the matter is important, to have such documents sent to Costa Rica for study in draft form.

Cuba. See Chapter 9.

Czechoslovakia. See Chapter 9.

Denmark. Although there is no special legislation affecting agency agreements, it is worth the while of exporters to take note of what the Federation of Nordic Commercial Agents would like to see enforced world-wide. This would indicate to the foreign principal the basic terms that Scandinavian agents would consider as minimum requirements. (See page 107.)

Dominican Republic. This is another of those countries which has enacted legislation in order to safeguard the interests of its agency firms. It particularly aims at fair compensation for loss of an agency without just cause.

Unilateral termination of an agreement by the principal permits the agent to claim reparation for a long list of considerations. These include the efforts and expenses the agent invested in working on the principal's behalf; the expenses he incurred in buying or converting offices or other premises, tools, furniture, and installations in order to carry out the principal's business effectively; the value of goods, spare parts, and accessories including their transport on which he would have made a profit if the agreement had continued; and the profit he would have made if the agreement had not been prematurely terminated. If the exact period of future profitable business cannot be determined, then local courts can make judgement on this, taking as a basis for calculation the average annual profit during three consecutive years of operation, with the indemnity period being not more than five years.

It is also important to note that even where the principal terminates the contract on terms laid down in the agency agreement, he can still be called upon to pay compensation for the equipment and premises and stocks which the agent has invested in solely for the principal's business, on condition that the principal's method of exercising his right to terminate can be considered untimely, unexpected or capricious.

It is considered to be detrimental to the proper interests of the local agent if the principal terminates the agreement in order to set up local manufaturing facilities and the compensation terms then apply in the same way.

These regulations cannot be waived by private agreement as the Dominican Republic public law takes precedent.

Egypt. See United Arab Republic, page 114.

Formosa. See Taiwan, page 112.

France. There is some legal protection in France for agents who are dismissed prematurely. They are entitled to claim compensation even if the principal's action is justified for his own business reasons. Compensation is only inapplicable in those cases where dismissal is the result of a provable fault on the part of the agent.

This situation makes it particularly advisable for foreign exporters to see that a definite period for the duration of the agency is written into the agreement and to ensure that the period is not indefinitely prolonged by implied or tacit agreement.

If an agreement gives a commission agent the mandate to represent the principal it does not necessarily follow that it prohibits the agent from handling competitive goods. This has to be stated categorically within the terms of the agreement. It is possible for the agreement to specify a law other than that of France to be resorted to if a dispute arises.

Germany, East (Deutsche Demokratische Republik). See Chapter 9.

Germany, West (Bundesrepublik Deutschland). There is a German commercial code which makes certain provisions on the subject of agency agreements.

If there is no fixed period of duration for an agency contract, then it can be terminated within the first three years of its existence with six weeks' notice, to be calculated up to the end of a calendar quarter. If terms are laid down in the agreement, these cannot be less than a minimum of one complete calendar month.

The minimum notice is a full calendar quarter when an agency relationship has lasted more than three years.

An agent can claim commission on all transactions concluded during the period of his agency, and also on transactions concluded subsequently if these are the result mainly of negotiations carried out by him when agent.

In the absence of separate arrangements, the agent can claim payment of commission when the buyer settles the account with the principal.

If a principal terminates an agency without justifiable reason, the agent can normally claim compensation for future business benefits the principal will derive from the agent's work, this compensation amounting to not more than the value of a year's commission based on the average of the preceding five years, or on the total duration of the agency if less than five years.

It would appear possible for foreign law to apply in place of German law if an agency agreement is specifically made subject to the foreign principal's own national law.

Guinea. On the whole, commercial law in Guinea is based on the French code, but special decrees have been made to safeguard, in this instance, the interests of the state *vis-à-vis* business to be conducted with foreign principals.

Manufacturers are only allowed to appoint local agents when the products to be handled require after-sales service for their proper functioning. Permission must be granted by the Minister of Commerce, with applications being made jointly by the principal and the would-be agent. It must be made satisfactorily evident that the arrangement will result in an effective after-sales service for technical goods.

The agent can have exclusive importation rights except in connection with purchases by the state. The government's offices are at all times permitted to place direct orders and, in any circumstances, orders from government buying agencies and public utilities are not allowed to be the subject of commission of any kind for the local agent.

This does not apply to orders for spare parts, which can be handled exclusively by the agent.

Hungary. See Chapter 9.

Iraq. Like some other developing countries, Iraq has introduced laws which help to expand the amount of business processed by its own citizens. There is a policy of "Iraquisation" of trade as far as this is compatible with efficient commercial services.

Any representative, agent, or distributor must be an Iraqi resident in Iraq and he must register with his chamber of commerce so that he is entered in the Register of Commercial Agencies.

Exceptions can be made where some essential technical expertise or experience is required which is not possessed by Iraqis, so that foreign nationals are obliged to handle the agency to provide the necessary level of administration, maintenance, or servicing.

Italy. Italian regulations generally follow reasonable lines to safeguard the interests of principals and agents from harsh treatment by the other party. They uphold the right of agents to exclusive territorial agreements and they ensure that principals can insist on the agent's not operating on behalf of competitive products.

Unless there is a fixed period of duration of the agency agreement, then three months' notice must be given prior to termination of a contract. If the required notice is not given, then the agent can claim compensation up to one quarter of the commission earned in the previous twelve months, in lieu of notice. In addition he can also claim compensation if the termination of the contract is not reasonably justified.

There is a special semi-public social security agency, ENASARCO, which can receive annually a certain proportion of earned commission from the principal and the agent and which can then use the accumulated sum to reimburse an agent who is prematurely dismissed.

Agents are obliged to register their activities with their provincial chamber of commerce, giving details of all principals he represents and supplying a copy of each agency agreement he has entered into.

Generally, only Italian law is applicable to disputes between an Italian agent and a foreign principal. However, there is some lack of clarity regarding the definition of agent, representative, and distributor and in some instances foreign law clauses in an agreement might well be upheld. Local legal advice is essential at the outset.

Kuwait. All agents in Kuwait must be Kuwaiti nationals and they must be registered with the Ministry of Commerce. Then the following information is officially published concerning each registration: names and nationalities of both parties, description of goods to be handled, territory covered by the agency agreement, duration of agreement if for a fixed period, addresses of commercial offices of both parties and any trade names of goods being marketed.

The agency register is cross-indexed by name of agent, name of principal, type of goods, and trade names. This can be useful knowledge for prospective exporters.

Libya. This rapidly developing country, until recently one of the poorest in the world and now benefiting from rich oil strikes, has introduced legislation aimed at spreading business opportunities around a large number of enterprises.

In a country starting from such a backward position, a sudden influx of business could well have meant too large a proportion of it going into the hands of the very few people or firms with business experience.

Accordingly, the law prohibits any person or company from holding more than ten agencies. When the law was introduced in 1961, those operating on behalf of more than the prescribed maximum limit had to relinquish the excess to other firms. The law also prohibits people from holding partnerships in other firms if their total interests exceed ten agencies.

Only Libyan nationals may be appointed agents or representatives on behalf of foreign firms and they must be registered in the commercial register of their province. They must furnish proof that they have never been declared bankrupt and that they have never been convicted for infringements of the law governing commercial agents.

Documents must include a copy of the agreement with a foreign principal, details of the financial arrangements agreed between the parties and a declaration ensuring that the principal's currency can be converted into Libyan currency to meet the payment of these agreed terms.

If a joint venture acts as agent or representative, the company must have at least 51 per cent of its shares held by Libyan nationals.

Agents are only allowed to act directly on behalf of the principal or another agent located in the agent's own home country.

On those occasions when a product requires very specialised technical experience for efficient marketing, then permission may be granted by the Ministry of National Economy for the principal to appoint as agent or representative someone from his own home country for a period not exceeding one year. It is conditional, for the necessary approval, that one or more Libyans work with the agent in order to be trained to take over the agency at the end of a year.

New Zealand. A strict import licensing system means that only agents possessing the necessary licences can act on behalf of a foreign principal, otherwise he is not empowered to import the goods into New Zealand.

When an agency agreement is terminated, then the agent in New Zealand retains the licences for the type of product which has been handled. This enables him to act on behalf of a new principal in a similar field of operations, but it might mean that the former principal cannot continue his business in New Zealand, unless he is able to find another agent who also has permits to import his goods.

Norway. Although there is no specific legislation regarding agencies, there is in Norway a very influential Import and Export Agents Association which has a strict code of statutory provisions. Its regulations normally apply to dealings with all Norwegian agents.

One of the main provisions to watch is that which forbids any local agent to accept a new principal, if that principal has previously been represented by another firm, without first informing the original agent of the approach. This gives the first agent a chance to safeguard his own interests. It also means that if the principal attempts to break off an agency relationship in an unjustified manner, then he will find it extremely difficult, if not impossible, to find alternative representation. (See also Scandinavia, below.)

Poland. See Chapter 9.

Rumania. See Chapter 9.

Scandinavia. The Federation of Nordic Commercial Agents has worked on a draft for a proposal on international law submitted to it by the Swedish Agents Association. As this was intended to be found acceptable internationally, its provisions might well be regarded by exporters as summarising most of the points to be borne in mind when drafting agency agreements and certainly those which are likely to be taken as a minimum starting point when dealing with agents in Scandinavia.

Most of the items under discussion seem to be based on a common-sense approach to the protection of the interests of agent and principal on basic matters.

It is suggested that commission ought to be paid on all transactions when the purchaser has fulfilled his liabilities concerning payment. If only part of an order is completed and paid for, then the agent should receive commission in proportion. If an order is

107

not fully paid for but the cash received by the principal is more than the total he would have retained after paying commission, then the difference should be paid as commission to the agent. The agent should also be entitled to commission on contracts which are not fulfilled due to fault or negligence on the part of the principal.

Where an agent has sole selling rights in a specified territory, he is entitled to commission on any orders from that territory, irrespective of whether or not he has actually been involved in the negotiations.

An agent should receive a statement of orders on which he is entitled to commission on a quarterly basis, receiving payment due to him within fifteen days of the end of each quarter at the latest.

The agent is to be expected to act in his capacity to the best of his ability and also to keep his principal properly informed of any aspects of his market which might affect the principal's business. Similarly, the principal is to be expected to keep the agent informed if he has any reason to anticipate a decline in business in the agent's market. The principal is obliged to provide all necessary information and material to enable the agent to sell his products, such as price lists, samples, and patterns, if applicable. This does not necessarily include sales literature, the supply of which being a matter of agreement between the two parties.

If there is any claim by the agent for remuneration being withheld by the principal, then the agent should have the right of lien on samples, goods, patterns, or other property belonging to the principal which has come into the hands of the agent during his normal function.

Where the agent accepts *del credere* risk, becoming responsible for the part or complete payment by the end purchaser, then he should be granted a bigger commission than normal, or some other form of remuneration for the added responsibility.

Agents should not be entitled to accept payment for goods or services supplied by the principal unless specifically authorised by the principal to do so.

Agents should be entitled to some form of compensation proportionate to the amount of benefit the principal will derive after the termination of an agreement which can be traced to any sales or promotional efforts made by the agent during the period of the agreement. This assumes that the agreement is not unilaterally terminated by the agent.

Agency agreements should not prohibit the agent from entering into competition with the principal's goods for longer than two years after the end of the relationship. If any clause is included which restrains the agent's activities for a period after the agency is terminated, then some compensation ought to be paid to offset this hindrance to his business opportunities.

When an agency agreement has been in force for more than two years, then there should be a minimum period of notice for both sides of three months.

Claims for compensation by either party should be put forward not later than one year from the time when damage first came to light.

Sweden. Swedish law contains certain articles to govern disputes between agent and principal if the points at issue have not been covered in a private agency agreement. Furthermore, standard business practice would also be taken into account, which, to a great extent, would probably be reflected in the proposals put forward for international law by the Swedish Agents Association. (See Scandinavia, page 107.)

Swedish legal regulations are very explicit on the points which concern the obligations of the principal and the purchaser where there is an agent acting as intermediary. Where an agent concludes a contract with a purchaser on a principal's behalf which is outside the limit of his authority and which the principal does not wish to approve, then the latter must not delay in advising the purchaser, either directly or through the agent, otherwise it must automatically be assumed that the principal has given his approval to the contract.

Switzerland. As might be expected, Switzerland has a Federal Act which explicitly and in detail lays down the law on agency contracts. It states that where the sphere of activities of the agent is in Switzerland, the contract between agent and principal must be subject to the laws of Switzerland. These deal with the obligations of the agent, his authority, the obligations of the principal, termination of a contract, and claims for commission and compensation.

The legal rights of the agent with regard to *del credere* risk, restriction of trade, and termination of agency contract cannot be reduced or waived by private agreement.

An agent is required to safeguard the interests of the principal in a proper business-like manner, but he can act on behalf of other principals unless otherwise contracted.

He does not undertake liability for payments or for the fulfilment of other obligations by the customer and he cannot be expected to bear any part of the cost of collecting claims unless these duties are agreed in writing. In this instance, the agent has an inalienable claim to special remuneration proportionate to the risk or expense undertaken.

During an agency agreement and after its termination the agent may not exploit or divulge any business secrets of his principal which he has had access to during the agency relationship. If a clause is agreed in the agency agreement which prohibits the agent from any competitive business operation in the market, then he acquires an inalienable title to special compensation, proportionate to the damage ensuing to his business prospects.

The agent is not deemed entitled to receive payments, grant respites for payment, or agree any other contract changes without the principal's authorisation.

For his part, the principal is required to take all reasonable action to enable the agent to carry out his duties successfully, including supplying the agent with any necessary information. The principal is required to inform the agent wherever he wishes to curtail sales in the territory or whenever he foresees or anticipates any substantial reduction in business in the territory.

Where an agent has been allocated a definite area of operation, either by type of customer or geographical entity, then the agent can assume he has the sole right to business in that area unless agreement has been otherwise specified in writing.

The agent has the right to claim commission on all business negotiated by him during the agency period, and also on any transaction concluded by the principal with customers without the agent's negotiation if these customers have been introduced as potential business partners by the agent. If there is an exclusive agency agreement, then the agent is entitled to receive commission on all contracts within his area.

Commission is assumed to be legally earned as soon as sales contracts have become legally valid, but the agent's claim to commission can lapse if a contract is not carried out through no fault or negligence on the part of the principal.

In the absence of other agreed terms, then commission is due for payment at the end of each calendar half-year. The principal is obliged to provide the agent with a half-yearly written statement listing the orders subject to commission and to grant the agent facilities, if requested, for inspection of the books and documents backing the statement. The agent cannot waive his claim to this right in advance.

If a principal fails to carry out without cogent reason his contractual obligations, then he is required to pay the agent a sum commensurate with the commission he could have expected to earn.

Where an agency agreement has been in force for more than twelve months and where the agent is not permitted to act on another principal's behalf, he is entitled to receive compensation from the principal for a relatively short time if he is unable to perform his duties due to illness or due to compulsory military service in the Swiss armed forces. The compensation has to be commensurate with the loss of potential earnings and the agent is not permitted to waive this right in advance.

Although the agent cannot claim normal business expenses back from the principal unless previously agreed, he is entitled to reimbursement for cash laid out for items such as freight and customs duties connected with his principal's business.

To safeguard any outstanding claims or future claims for commission when there is a dispute or when the principal goes bankrupt, the agent is entitled to retain any properties or money he holds on behalf of the principal as a result of his agency duties. Price lists and lists of customers are excluded from his right of retention.

If a specific time limit is set for an agency duration, then no notice is required to terminate when the time expires.

However, if the agency relationship is tacitly continued after the specified period is ended, then the contract between agent and principal is deemed to have been renewed for the same term or for one year, whichever is the shorter. If notice is required in order to terminate an agreement and if neither side gives notice, then the agreement is deemed to be renewed.

If there is no specific term of duration and no laid down terms of giving notice, then during the first year of a relationship notice to terminate should be a full calendar month. Agencies of longer

111

duration can be terminated at the end of a calendar quarter with two months' prior notice, unless otherwise agreed. All terms must be identical for both principal and agent.

For cogent reasons either side can terminate the agreement at any time, provisions being the same as for contracts of service.

An agency relationship can be said to expire on the death of the agent or the bankruptcy of the principal. In the event of the death of the principal, the agency relationship only terminates if the contract was entered into materially in respect of his person.

According to Swiss rulings, unless there is something in writing to the contrary then the agent has no claim to commission on any repeat orders from his customers after the agency agreement has terminated. However, there are occasions when the agent can claim compensation in respect of profit to be gained from his work by the principal after the end of their relationship. The claim cannot exceed one year's average earnings calculated on the basis of the previous five years, or the whole of the period if the agency relationship was not in existence for so long. The agent cannot, though, make any claims for compensation if he himself brings the relationship to a close.

Taiwan (Formosa). The terms of the special regulations in Taiwan to control agents are very rigid and in many instances unique. It is not difficult to guess at the potential misdemeanours they are intended to prevent. Fundamentally they would appear to be protecting the state's access to foreign currency earnings, avoiding the possibility of unscrupulous agents benefiting from import monopolies and ensuring that public authorities are able to buy at the most competitive price.

Agents come under the control of the Foreign Exchange and Trade Control Commission, FETCC, with which they must be registered, submitting, amongst other documents, the original and a photostat of the agency agreement with the foreign principal.

The agreement has to be in some detail, covering the date, duration, and means of termination of the agency, the names, brands, and specifications of products to be handled, the list price and the net price to the agent with instructions on how the agent is to issue quotations. There must be complete information on how commission is to be assessed and how and when paid. Assurance has to be given that whenever there is a price increase notified, then existing quotations will still be recognised. The agreement has to state expressly that the principal affords the sole rights in Taiwan to the agent and that he has studied and confirmed all the regulations.

The FETCC publishes a register of approved agents and the products they handle.

Imports are only allowed into Taiwan on licence and this is only granted when the application is accompanied by a copy of the quotation submitted by the approved agent. No other source of the identical commodities is acceptable unless there is a price advantage in foreign currency terms; that is, the quoted price being less than the net price to the agent. Agents are not allowed to quote higher prices than those registered as list prices nor lower than those registered as net to him, except where they are competing in open tender and there are special instructions from the principal.

Delivery dates quoted must be the shortest for the first inquirer. It is not permissible to give any special favour on delivery date to subsequent potential customers.

There are also rigid conditions for the issuing of quotations. These have to specify, among other items, name, brand, and packing method of the product, quantity, unit price, and total price of the product, with the total price broken down to show the sums for freight, insurance, and net cost of goods. It is up to the buyer to determine whether to purchase f.a.s., f.o.b., c. and f., or c.i.f. The quotation must also indicate the means of shipment, by air, sea, or post, giving port of origin, port of delivery and date of shipping.

Agents are strictly forbidden to accept any rebate other than agreed commission from the foreign supplier or to allow any rebate or commission to the buyer.

Foreign principals are expected to remit the earned commission to the agent within one month of the conclusion of the contracted business and the agent is obliged to exchange this at an authorised bank forthwith. The agents must also submit a detailed return twice-yearly of all commissions earned and cash exchanged. If the agency requires foreign currency in order to promote its own business by sending its staff abroad, then they are allowed to apply for not more than 40 per cent of their foreign exchange earnings.

There are severe penalties for infringements of these regulations, from suspension for three months to complete and permanent loss of all agency registrations and trading licences.

It is incumbent upon the foreign principal to complete a supplier's certificate on receipt of payments, indicating the amount of commission being paid to the agent. If the foreign principal defaults on payment of the commission, then all his agency registrations will be revoked and all current trade transactions with him will be suspended.

United Arab Republic (Egypt). The UAR has taken many steps towards the socialisation of the country, placing the exclusive responsibility for international trade in the hands of government or semi-government organisations. Only approved registered firms can act as agents on behalf of foreign principals and these firms must be government companies or general organisations in which the government has at least a 25 per cent holding.

These recognised agency firms must register all their agency agreements with the Commercial Registration and Control Administration, stating the terms of the contracts, the duration of their validity, the exclusive rights agreed, and the products to be handled.

Yugoslavia. See Chapter 9.

USSR. See Chapter 9.

When the State is the Agent

This chapter discusses agency systems in the centrally planned republics of Bulgaria, China, Cuba, Czechoslovakia, East Germany, Hungary, Poland, Rumania, Yugoslavia, and USSR. In these communist countries all means of production, distribution and international trade are owned by the state. This means that whether one is exporting to industry or to distributors for the consumer public, the orders are placed by state-owned organisations. In these countries, the state does not allow any local citizens to act as middlemen, taking a profit on state transactions. If any agencies are allowed at all (generally they are not), then these are also state organisations set up to fulfil some of the functions of sales representatives on behalf of foreign companies.

THE BASIC SYSTEM

Not many months ago the basic system would have been a near-enough true description of the practice in each of the communist countries, with only very small local differences. Now, however, major reforms have been introduced in Czechoslovakia and Hungary and, to a certain extent, in the USSR and Bulgaria. It is still essential to understand the background principles in order to be able to appreciate the new distinctions and interpret the changes which are being introduced rapidly to rectify some of the faults in the previous systems.

When all business was nationalised in a communist take-over of the government of a country, private profit was completely abolished as a motivation or as an objective. The principle was "to each according to his needs; from each according to his ability."

When profit was abolished at all levels, the new target was the benefit of the state.

Accordingly state committees were set up to regulate every aspect of economic life, evaluating ideas, making plans on a national scale in a way which was believed to make the most efficient use of all the country's resources—of raw materials, production facilities and manpower and, of course, foreign exchange.

All economic activities were reorganised on a vertical basis, with branches of industry and commerce reporting up towards government bodies. Thus, light engineering factories were controlled by a Ministry of Light Engineering; chemical plants were controlled by a Ministry of Chemical Production. Poland alone has fifteen industrial ministries, whilst the USSR has almost fifty. Soviet ministries include:

> All Union Ministry for Engineering, for Light and Food Industries, and Domestic Appliances
> All Union Ministry for General Engineering
> All Union Ministry for Heavy, Power, and Transport Engineering
> All Union Ministry for Instrument Building, Means of Automation, and Control Systems
> All Union Ministry for Medium Engineering
> All Union Ministry for the Radio Industry
> All Union Ministry for the Shipbuilding Industry
> All Union Ministry for Tractor and Agricultural Engineering

These ministries are only responsible for the production of the categories of goods in their factories. When told what the state plans are for their industry, they tell what materials and machines they require to meet the given targets and then their job is to ensure that their factories produce the budgeted output.

The design of equipment and plant is the responsibility of another group of state organisations—the central planning and design offices.

In Poland for example, these include:

> Central Office for Ball and Roller Bearing Construction
> Central Office for Cable Construction

116

Central Office for the Construction of Machinery and
  Equipment for the Peat Industry
Meat Industry Projects Office
Motor-car Industry Construction Office
Railway Electrification Projects Office
Rubber Industry Projects Office
Studies and Projects Office for Communications

Similarly, research is centralised at institutes catering specifically
for different branches of industry, with co-ordinated control to
avoid overlapping.

It will be noted that none of these organisations are responsible
for selling or buying anything. They are there to meet requirements but not to create demand or to investigate the nature of
demand. They are almost entirely production orientated.

The factories receive targets they have to meet and are issued
with the raw materials, equipment, and components they need to
produce the goods.

The international commercial aspects of the business, buying
and selling, are handed over to state trading companies. Generally
each trading company has the monopoly right to import and export goods in specific categories. If we take machine tools as an
example, the following trading enterprises have sole right to
purchase machine tools from abroad:

Bulgaria	Machinoimport
China	China National Machinery Import and Export Corporation
Cuba	Maquimport
Czechoslovakia	Strojimport
East Germany	WMW-Export
Hungary	Technoimpex
Poland	Metalexport
Rumania	Masinimport
Yugoslavia	Invest-Import (Belgrade)
	Masino-Impex (Zagreb)
	Metalka (Ljubljana)
	Metalexport (Sarajevo)
	Note: Many Yugoslav enterprises operate on a regional basis
USSR	Stankoimport

The fact that the word "export" appears in the title of some of the enterprises responsible for imports should not cause confusion. Since their foundation many of the trading companies have evolved, taking over additional functions or swapping responsibilities with others. For example, in Czechoslovakia the foreign trade corporation called Strojexport ("machinery export") originally specialised only in the export of almost all types of Czechoslovak machinery, whilst Strojimport handled the purchasing from abroad of all the country's equipment requirements. Later it was thought that it would be more efficient to have each enterprise handling two-way trade in a more specialised range of equipment, so that Strojimport now handles import and export of machine tools, whilst Strojexport handles import and export of plant such as road-making machinery and electric motors and heavy plant. Strojexport has also been divided into two, with a new enterprise called Pragoinvest formed to handle import and export of ranges of capital equipment such as generators, locomotives, and gearboxes.

It is important to appreciate that the names of these enterprises no longer necessarily describe their exact spheres of activities, for many errors have been made as a result of misunderstandings over names. One British firm was about to make a final visit to Prague to negotiate an order for clean air plant and could not manage to get their Czechoslovak contacts to respond. The reason was that all the telex messages had been forwarded by an over-helpful girl in Lancashire who had "corrected" Strojexport (the potential importer of the plant) to Strojimport, a company which had not the faintest idea what the telexes were all about.

Furthermore, as these portmanteau words are a favourite method of naming state corporations in the communist countries, many do tend to sound alike, adding to the potential confusion. Elektroimpex with a *k* is in Hungary, whilst Electroimpex with a *c* is in Bulgaria, both handling import and export of various kinds of electrical plant. Bulgaria has a Machinoexport and the Soviet Union has one too, whilst Rumania has a foreign trade company with an identically sounding name, spelt Masinexport. The new Czechoslovak company Pragoinvest should not be confused with the slightly longer established company Investa, Prague, nor with the East German organisation Invest-Export.

Obviously there are not so many of these trading companies

that there can be a special one for each different type of product handled. There are only about forty in the Soviet Union, the same number in Poland and East Germany, and only eighteen in Rumania. The result is that they all have to take on wide ranges of goods in addition to the major lines which might have initiated their official names. Elektroimpex of Hungary, for example, used to handle not only electronic and telecommunication equipment, which one would expect from its title, but also vacuum flasks. Merkuria, a recently established Czechoslovak enterprise, handles imports and exports of engineers' hand tools, enamelled hollow-ware, microscopes and photographic enlargers, hotel and restaurant equipment and the kitchen sink (of anodised aluminium).

However, it is not too difficult to discover which state enterprise is responsible for the purchase of one's own type of product. The embassies, trade delegations, and trade offices of the communist countries are extremely helpful in putting would-be exporters in touch with their counterparts in the capital back home. They can usually give the name and address of the relevant company or quickly find it out on behalf of anyone who makes a request.

Many of the embassies have active trade delegations which are often staffed with representatives from the major trading enterprises. These executives act as liaison officers, seeking suppliers for goods their companies wish to import, and appointing agents and helping sales on behalf of the products their companies are trying to export. They are also informed in advance of any buying delegations planning to visit their territory, so that local exporters may frequently have the opportunity of meeting people from the state importing companies on their own home ground, possibly arranging for them to call at their factories to see goods being produced.

Still dealing with the "basic system," it must be pointed out that it is the job of the importing enterprises to buy what has been planned by other organisations, by the state committees, and by the other ministries. They know well in advance, according to one-year and five-year plans, what sort of goods they have to purchase and in what quantities. They can, therefore, inform a manufacturer whether or not there is any chance at all that his goods might be purchased. If there is a chance, because the plan allows it, then it is a matter of hard bargaining on quality, price, and delivery, for the enterprise will have offers from many parts of the world and will have had business experience with scores of foreign suppliers.

The foreign trade enterprises were generally responsible not to the industrial ministries whose factories used the equipment they purchased, or manufactured the goods they exported, or retailed the consumer articles they bought; they were responsible to the Ministry of Foreign Trade which controlled the international dealings of the country as a whole. The defect of the basic system, as seen by several of the countries which are reforming their economic structure, was that the trading companies acted as too much of an insulator between world markets and home producers. There was no interaction with foreign industries, and no pressures or incentives from the outside world of business acted upon the home industries. Not price, but output was the governing factor, not profitability or productivity, but increased production to meet the targets—at the expense of high costs and inadequate quality.

The changes now taking place are aimed at making the home economy more sensitive to outside influences, so that there is an element of competition. Previously things were only imported if they could not be made in the home country or could not be made in sufficient quantity from local sources. The domestic factories have to consider price and productivity and in several of the countries the profit motive has been introduced. The factory managements have to make a profit to pay wages, meet the cost of their materials, and cover the cost of capital investment and working finance. They have been given the responsibility of specifying their own machinery and have been given the right of access to foreign exchange, based upon the amount they earn as exporters.

Whereas the earlier system placed all the foreign currency for imports in the hands of the trading companies, now, in Czechoslovakia and Hungary especially, the factories, the state hotel groups, and the consumer distribution organisations have been given the use of their own foreign earnings, or the right to buy foreign exchange (at a very high price), for the importation of the goods they feel they need from abroad. This movement is far advanced in Czechoslovakia and Hungary, beginning to be introduced in the Soviet Union and Bulgaria, a certain way along the road in East Germany (German Democratic Republic) and is the system which has, in fact, been operating for some time in Yugoslavia. Recent events in Czechoslovakia were partly because of Soviet opinion that this type of reform was moving too rapidly.

Yugoslavia, although a country where all industry and resources are "social property," needs special attention, because its management organisation has been different to the other socialist states of East Europe. The social property is under the self-management of the people employed by each organisation through workers' councils which elect the boards of management.

There is not the same allocation of monopoly rights as in the other communist territories, for each enterprise which is set up becomes autonomous.

Overall control of the economy is achieved through a loose five-year plan system which lays down the objectives the state hopes to reach and priorities which should be heeded by the federal and individual republican governments, by the banks and the major enterprises. In addition, imports are controlled by a six-category system classifying everything as free import, or free with certain conditions, or permissible within a global currency quota, or within a specific currency quota, or within a quota for a specific commodity or by special import licence.

The manufacturing enterprises can purchase products on their own account, especially if they earn currency by exporting. However, there are specialised trading companies which handle import or export or two-way trade in specific product lines on behalf of the end-users or the producers in Yugoslavia. There are more than 400 of these, with competitors in each field of activity. Some are specialised in importing on behalf of firms in their own republic, others handle goods for the whole of the federation.

THE AGENCY SITUATION

Nowadays the exporter wishing to sell to the communist countries must locate the relevant trading company and, at the same time, determine the extent to which the particular country has liberalised its economy. How much direct say in the purchase of his products is now vested in the end-user? In China, the exporter will have very little chance to sell direct to any end-user. All transactions are rigidly channelled through the monopoly corporation. But in Czechoslovakia it might mean negotiating with a factory group which is specifying the equipment, and simultaneously with the state trading company which will be handling the commercial transaction when the products have been approved. In Hungary it might mean doing the complete deal with, say, the Hungarian Shipyards and Crane Works or with the Tatabanya Mines, two of the forty or so big production units which now have the right to import directly a number of their special requirements.

Although the trading companies are the official import houses, they can in no way be regarded as agents for the foreign manufacturer. They act entirely to the benefit of their own state, buying as economically as possible from the most suitable source.

State Agencies. Four countries, only, make any provision for the representation of foreign suppliers in their territory. These are Yugoslavia, Poland, Hungary, and East Germany, and they do this by means of state-established agency companies which can look after foreign principals' interests.

Yugoslavia, with the greatest measure of independent action for its commercial and industrial undertakings, has over fifty such agency firms. Poland has nine, Hungary has just started a new system with eight authorised agencies and East Germany has a single one, Transinter GmbH. (The names of the official agencies in all these countries appear in Appendix 5.)

These agencies operate on a commission basis and are allowed to hold stocks on consignment which can be warehoused by the agencies without duty being paid until they are sold.

In Hungary the functions of the new agencies there are described as follows:

1   "Negotiation of sales of export and import goods between sellers and buyers
2   Technical and commercial publicity
3   Maintenance of commissioned consignments and sample stores
4   Market research
5   Organisation of technical shows, demonstrations, and symposiums"

(Hungarian Exporter, January 1968)

Agencies in eastern Europe charge commission rates which are negotiable with the foreign principal and which depend upon the amount of aid and the range of services desired. Their operations are becoming more flexible, so that it is sometimes possible to select an individual local citizen as the person best qualified to represent one's interests and arrange for him to be employed on one's behalf by a state agency. In these circumstances the man is paid a wage by the agency firm, which collects commission on all sales in the market, but the exporter can have direct access to the salesman, working with him, briefing him, and discussing sales policy with him.

The state agencies can also arrange, in return for a fee, to make office accommodation, secretarial services, and interpreters available to foreign exporters. It is very valuable to have people on the spot watching over one's interests, for it is a market in which buying personnel move fairly frequently from one department to another, so that lines of communication with a client can easily become disjointed. Frequently, too, the visiting salesman from abroad finds it difficult to decide whether or not he is really in touch with the executives who can make a decision, whether a "no" is really the end of the line or simply an attempt at a brush-off, whether difficult negotiations mean that they are more interested in some other firm's offer or whether they are simply trying to manœuvre him into a special discount.

Experience and detailed knowledge of the market are invaluable, so that the state agencies can be an aid. But, and this is a very big reservation, the agencies are, just like the trading companies and the end-users in the country, all state-owned and state-controlled. It is not as easy to see them as wholly devoted to the exporter's interests as a private agent in the western world, for example. It can be assumed that they will work hard to further the principal's sales prospects *vis-à-vis* those of another foreign competitor, in order to earn commission, but they cannot be entirely relied upon to negotiate the best possible terms for the principal *vis-à-vis* the state purchaser, unless the local salesman involved has been completely integrated into the exporter's whole effort by dint of a long period of close co-operation. That is where the personal relationship can count for a great deal.

Strategic Location of Outside Agents. An alternative agency arrangement employed by many exporters to the communist countries of Eastern Europe is to appoint representatives in near-by Western countries to tackle the markets on their behalf.

A favourite location is Vienna, very convenient for regular short trips to Budapest and Bucharest and to Prague and Brno,

A West German agent can also tackle these areas and be within fairly easy reach of Warsaw and Poznan and the business centres of East Germany.

If this system is adopted, it has to be remembered that communist state buyers are notoriously suspicious of all intermediaries, firmly convinced that their existence merely adds to the cost of the goods being sold. It is almost possible to see them calculate mentally the increased percentages which they will be paying out indirectly to private middlemen in Germany or Austria when they are supposed to be importing goods from the USA or the UK or Canada.

There are many occasions when they have made it very plain that they will only negotiate direct with the manufacturers.

It is therefore wise to ensure constant personal visits to the markets by head office staff (the more senior the better) even if the market is watched for opportunities and changes by a neighbouring agent. It is fatal to allow the potential buyers there to get the impression that the manufacturer is very remote from the business on hand.

Two-way Merchanting. An exception to the resentment felt by East Europeans towards intermediaries are the well-established export houses with a sound history of trade with the various republics.

These firms exist in the UK, Holland, France, Germany, and Austria and other countries. Their main strength lies in the fact that they not only help to sell foreign goods to the communist countries, but they do a considerable amount of business in purchases for the West from the East. They are looked upon with favour because they help these countries to earn quite large amounts of badly needed hard currency.

One trading firm, for example, handles vast quantities of East German chemicals, mainly potash. Another is Poland's biggest customer for ham. Others are agents in Western countries for Polish machine tools and Bulgarian tomatoes.

This two-way trade flow often allows them to arrange their transactions in such a way that the East European communist countries can buy what they need with a reduced foreign currency commitment, with proportions of the payments being made up of barter exchanges or "compensation" deals. These can be worked out on a multilateral basis, with, say, British cranes going to Hungary, Hungarian machine tools being delivered to Sweden and Swedish steel going to Britain, all through a central merchant or export house.

The British Export Houses Association in London or the exporter's chamber of commerce or government trade office should be able to effect an introduction to a suitable merchant.

Specialist Export Sales Agencies. Because communist countries require a depth of experience on the part of the exporter if progress is to be made, a number of people have set up specialist sales services. These range from an individual (sometimes a former émigré who speaks one or more of the local languages) handling several accounts simultaneously on his regular tours of the capitals and trade fairs of the communist territories, to sizeable organisations which mount special shows and demonstrations or joint exhibition stands on behalf of a variety of non-competitive manufacturers. If they operate under their own names they stand the chance of being held at arms length as mere intermediate commission hunters. Often, though, they act in the name of their principal, being appointed as part and parcel of the manufacturer's export department. In these instances they introduce themselves as employees of the principal, with visiting cards and notepaper all bearing the name of the foreign manufacturer. Their success depends, of course, upon the sales ability and personality of the executives who undertake the tours and personal sales visits. They can relieve the manufacturer of a lot of the burden of long, patient (or impatient) approaches before final business negotiations begin to materialise.

The introductory period, sometimes as long as two years (waiting for the next relevant plan to be formulated), has seen the breaking of many a hopeful exporter's patience, and because his endurance and determination have dwindled before contracts have been signed he has written off the investment to date and gone in search of more immediate business in other markets.

The investment in time and money can be greater than many firms are willing to risk, yet the fruits can be well worth the effort, for most of the potential customers, when they do buy, place orders on behalf of their whole country, often worth millions of pounds or tens of millions of dollars.

125

For this reason the British Government and ten leading British finance houses have seen fit to set up a new organisation with a special department which can develop Eastern European markets on behalf of British firms, endowing it with the necessary resources of cash and know-how.

Called the Overseas Marketing Corporation, with investment backing from the shareholders and loan capital from the Government, it has an Eastern European section which actually does the selling—of selected products which research shows to have the best opportunities over there. Qualified staff, with knowledge of local purchasing patterns and speaking local languages, make frequent sales visits to the areas, introducing new products, negotiating contracts, and exploring future needs. It is probably agencies of this scale which will be the pattern for the future as more governments see that their individual exporters will lose out on these big markets unless fully-fledged marketing is organised for them.

CHAPTER 10

The Unique Trading Companies of Japan

It would take a brave, or foolish, man to attempt to define the meaning of the British Commonwealth or the significance of American Primaries.

The same is true of any attempt to clarify the functions of Japan's trading companies. If they did not exist, no one could invent them. They have grown as an organic part of the nation and, like giant trees, if dissected, their layers of development reflect the variations of economic climate through the ages.

The answer to the question about how many trading companies there are in Japan depends upon the person being asked. If he is a Japanese government statistician he might reply—6200. If he is a high-ranking Japanese businessman he would probably reply—twelve. If he is an employee of one of the twelve he will almost certainly reply—one! Loyalty to one's company is an unrivalled Japanese phenomenon.

The figure of 6200 is that of a census report on the number of companies in Japan engaged in import-export business. However, of these about 4200 had an average turnover of less than £5000 ($12 000) per annum. Then came middle-sized firms with up to £5 million ($12 million) turnover, leaving about twelve mammoth trading companies with annual figures over or approaching the astronomical sum of £1000 million, or $2400 million—each.

Those dozen firms account for almost 70 per cent of Japan's total imports, almost 60 per cent of her total exports and 25 per cent of the country's wholesale domestic trade. There is nothing like this anywhere else in the world of business, for even in countries where all commerce is nationalised, there are no organisations handling such a comprehensive range of goods and equipment. The Japanese trading giants do not specialise in any commodities. They import and export nuts and bolts, noodles and nuclear power stations—each one of them in competition with the others.

There are four leaders within the big twelve. These are:

Mitsubishi Shoji Kaisha (literally "three-diamond trading company")
Mitsui Bussan
Marubeni-Iida
C Itoh

The other eight are:

Ataka and Company
Gosho Company
Iwai and Company
Kanematsu
Nichimen
Nissho
Sumitomo Shoji Kaisha
Toyo Menka Kaisha

Mitsubishi Shoji and Mitsui each have about 8000 employees, staffing about seventy overseas offices and subsidiaries and perhaps forty branch offices throughout Japan.

The major trading companies are represented in the world's business centres.

For example, there are Japanese subsidiaries or branch offices throughout the USA, in New York, Chicago, Los Angeles, San Francisco, Seattle, Portland, Houston, New Orleans, Dallas, St Louis, Honolulu, and Washington DC.

In Canada one or more of the companies have offices in Vancouver, Toronto, and Montreal.

In Europe they can be found with substantial companies or offices in London, Milan, Paris, Dusseldorf, Hamburg, Brussels, Amsterdam, Vienna, Madrid, and even Moscow.

Perhaps their main strength is in the countries of South-East Asia, in the Philippines, Malaysia, Hong Kong, Korea, Thailand, Taiwan, Burma, Indonesia, and India. As Japanese trade increases with Australia, so there is a growth of trading companies' establishments there, with offices already busy in Sydney, Melbourne, Brisbane, Perth, and Fremantle.

Japan made a late entry into capitalism. By the time the country had made the decision to become a modern industrial nation, others in Europe and America had already established companies with good financial backing in every category.

Japan had to rely on the funds which could be made available from a few powerful banks. These invested in manufacturing plants and put additional finance into trading companies to handle the manufactured goods on world and home markets.

After the Second World War, when the Mitsubishi and Mitsui "zaibatsu" were considered too powerful as independent entities and were broken down into smaller production and trading units, there was a complex re-alignment of banks, trading firms, and factories, so that a number of new groups emerged with a confused permutation of inter-connections.

Simultaneously, with the rapid advance of Japanese technology in many fields, numbers of new factories grew to international status outside the immediate influence of the banks or the trading companies. However, following traditional outlooks, the tendency was for the manufacturers to concentrate almost exclusively on production, using the services of existing trading organisations to market the products on world markets and to seek and purchase the raw materials and components needed for their production programmes. When capital was required for expansion, the banks and the trading companies invested in the factories. Many of the industrialists invested their profits in the shares of the trading firms which represented them, producing the present-day situation where, apparently, a team of expert American financial journalists tried to study the question of who owns what in the Mitsubishi Group and had to give up in bewilderment.

Taking Mitsubishi as an example, here is a list of some of the twenty-two major firms in the overall group:

Mitsubishi Heavy Industries
Mitsubishi Electric
Mitsubishi Shipbuilding
Mitsubishi Chemical Machinery
Mitsubishi Paper Mills

Mitsubishi Mining
Mitsubishi Cement
Mitsubishi Plastic Industries
Mitsubishi Oil
Mitsubishi Steel Manufacturing
Mitsubishi Monsanto Chemical
Mitsubishi Metal Mining
Asahi Glass
Asahi Beer
Mitsubishi Rayon
Mitsubishi Chemical Industries
Mitsubishi Petrochemical
Mitsubishi Reynolds
Mitsubishi Atomic Power Industries

A Mitsubishi employee can drive a Mitsubishi car, travel in a company-made bus, buy gasoline from his firm's chain of gasoline stations, drink the group's beer whilst wearing clothes made from their own synthetic fibres, the raw materials having been carried in bulk cargo ships built in the Mitsubishi yards, using home-made steel. At home, his electric fan, refrigerator, scooter, washing machine, and the very building materials for the house, not to mention the excavators and bulldozers used to build it, can all have come from group factories.

At the centre of the group's finance is the Mitsubishi Bank.

The trading company, Mitsubishi Shoji, can be regarded as part of the overall group, yet only 30·7 per cent of its business is concerned with Mitsubishi products and it handles only 34·8 per cent of the group's output. Naturally, the word "only" in this context is curious, for that amounts to a very large turnover, but it shows that the trading companies do not have any monopoly rights in the distribution of their associate companies' goods.

The same is true of the other giant groups. Mitsui Bussan, the trading company, is part of a group with over thirty manufacturing associates, product for product vying in every field with Mitsubishi, even in nuclear power stations, bulk carriers and petrochemical complexes. Mitsui Bussan itself has more than 50 per cent holdings in about sixty companies and is represented on the boards of about 160. It handles, however, only 19·1 per cent of its group's output, making up only 19·9 per cent of its own trading turnover.

Sumitomo Shoji is the trading company affiliated to the Sumitomo Group of ten industrial firms. Yet it was Sumitomo Shoji which sold a $17 million thermal power plant to Indonesia for Mitsubishi Heavy Industries!

AID TO FOREIGN EXPORTERS

The lessons to be learnt from this brief review of the make-up of the Japanese trading companies are:

1   They control a very large slice of the Japanese market
2   They are accessible in most parts of the world
3   They can handle almost any product
4   They have an especially good entrée to their own group companies
5   It is possible for any single trading company to cut across group structures to deal with rival groups
6   They have the network and finance to reach any sector of the Japanese market on behalf of foreign goods

The trading company Nissho has acted as agent for McDonnell Aircraft of America to sell jet fighters to the Japanese defence force. C Itoh were their rivals, selling jet fighters on behalf of Northrop. Marubeni-Iida took on the job of introducing Ford Motor of the USA to Japan, whilst C Itoh handled Chrysler's interests. Mitsui Bussan acted for General Electric and it was Mitsubishi Shoji which represented Westinghouse.

Whereas it was thought that as Japan developed as an industrial nation, the trading companies would become an anachronism, the opposite has happened. The trading companies have kept right up to date, shaping their services to meet the needs of modern economies. To a large degree they see themselves as an integral part of the nation's structure and accept moral responsibility, like the patriarchal leaders they are, for the general welfare of the country's economy. They operate on very low export commissions for Japanese products, often as little as 1 per cent. Even imports are handled at little more than 2 per cent profit, whilst domestic transactions are said to average at about 4 per cent profit. They contribute part of their profits earned in underdeveloped countries to a fund which subsidises the import of high-priced commodities from the poorer nations. This makes it possible for the trading companies to buy raisins from Iran, dates from Iraq and cotton from Nigeria at rates which would otherwise be prohibitive. They also invest capital in plant in underdeveloped countries to produce goods they can later sell in Japan or other markets, increasing their own business and contributing to the growth of the primitive industries.

TECHNICAL KNOW-HOW IMPORTS

Far from suffering from the technical advance of Japanese industry, the trading companies have contributed greatly to its development. "Invisible" imports of licences and know-how have become an important part of their international business. Several of the companies have set up specialised technical offices in Japan to act as clearing houses for licences, with executives being trained in this form of transaction. Offices have been set up in places such as New York, London, and Dusseldorf (by Mitsui for example) to locate suitable manufacturers and negotiate licence exchanges and sales. The commission on such a transaction is by no means the main objective for the trading companies. They often arrange to obtain sole rights for the marketing of the products to be manufactured under the agreement. They also try to secure the rights to import any materials needed in the manufacturing process.

Licence agreements are now very big business in Japan. There is an average of 750 know-how agreements per annum negotiated to be of more than one-year duration. Approximately two-thirds of these are with American firms, one-tenth with West Germany and about 5 per cent with UK companies. They have mainly concerned heavy engineering, chemical production, and electrical machinery, but there is a growing trend now towards licence purchases for consumer goods and light industrial products.

The trading companies, as in other fields, are handling licences not only for their own immediate groups but also for the enormous number of very small independent Japanese firms which have no organisation to cope with deals outside Japan but which are trying hard to modernise. It is said there are 60 000 Japanese companies which do not even have the facility to write a letter in anything but

Japanese. (And that is a very laborious business: Japanese type-writers have to be fitted with over 2000 characters!)

There are more and more instances of the trading giants going even further. They are not only locating valuable technical know-how and willing Japanese manufacturers, but they are themselves entering intro tripartite partnerships with a Western company to supply know-how, a Japanese factory to provide the manufactur-ing facilities and their own finance and distribution facilities to complete the picture.

THIRD MARKET TRANSACTIONS

There is another aspect of the services which Japan's unparalleled traders can offer to foreign industrialists. They have successfully made use of their world-wide networks to act as intermediaries between second and third markets—transactions which bypass Japan altogether. The present estimate is that about 3 per cent of their business is now in deals which do not involve a Japanese buyer or seller, and they are in a mood to double this. The figures are even more significant for some of the foreign stations, with over 50 per cent of one European office's turnover stemming from its business with markets where it has strong connections, excluding Japan.

Japanese trading firms are now selling South-East Asian rubber to the USA, Australian sugar to Indonesia. Brazilian peppermint to Europe and Formosan pineapples to the USA and Europe.

Dangers.   Because of their size, the Japanese trading companies tend to swallow up exporters who are not big enough to demand special attention. If the firm is not a Ford or a Chrysler there is a danger of the sales effort flagging for lack of impetus to drive it right through the trading company and out the other end.

They are very much departmentalised, so that there are textile sections, machine tool sections, canned food sections, and so on to offer specialist services in these different categories, but a manufacturer has to prepare his ground extremely carefully before placing his Japanese business entirely in their hands. It is as well to check beforehand the amount of effort the company is willing to put into the sales programme. It is also necessary to ensure that they come forward with a small research survey to indicate the potential outlets in Japan which they are entirely competent to reach.

At times it could be possible to work through more than one trading company with differently formulated exclusive rights for each. One might accept the task of introducing the product to a listed number of clients with whom it has special relations, whilst another undertakes a separate list of clients. Exclusivity is not a Japanese tradition. Even their advertising agencies handle competitive clients under the same roof and the clients themselves do not necessarily restrict themselves always to the same agency, but give different agencies the chance to tender for individual campaigns, often switching here and there as the fancy or an attractive idea takes them.

It is perfectly justifiable, therefore, to approach more than one trading company and, if you have a worth-while product to offer, to allow them to compete for the business.

At the same time it must not be forgotten that other possible agency channels do exist, especially the old-established Western merchant houses which have handled two-way trade with Japan for many decades.

However, if the product to be exported or the licence to be sold has a big future in Japan's 100-million population market, it is not a bad thing to make a direct approach to the giants which have so much of that market in their gargantuan pockets.

CHAPTER 11

In Praise of Regional Agents

The earlier part of this book strongly recommended the exporter to select "key markets" and cultivate them intensively, rather than dot the map with little meaningless flags of representation. "Vanity agents" are those which are appointed because it looks good on the company notepaper or because an overseas agent made a tour in your area and flattered you by asking for your account.

However, one can be enjoying a false sense of security if one has simply set up one agent in each major potential market. Experience shows that in many instances one agent is not enough per country. Export markets must not be defined by frontiers alone. They must be marked out on the sales map according to several other factors, which might be:

1   Geographical accessibility
2   Linguistic unity
3   Sheer limit of size
4   Regional differences in taste or tradition
5   Local media coverage
6   Range of agents' contacts
7   Location of agents' facilities

There are many misconceptions about "groups of markets" according to where the exporter comes from. Europeans, for example, might be satisfied with an "American" agent in New York, when local manufacturers would merely regard him as serving the East Coast. Australians, accustomed to viewing the States from another direction, are known to prefer their "American" agent in San Francisco, whereas local firms again would regard him as merely serving the South-West or only California.

Australians also imagine that it is possible to have a "Scandinavian" agent, perhaps in Stockholm or Copenhagen, whereas every country in Scandinavia requires at least one agent of its own and, in places such as Bergen and Oslo, it is usually much more efficient to have a separate agent for a particular local region.

The word "United" in United Kingdom should be a reminder to foreign manufacturers that the UK consists of more than one region. It is unlikely that the normal agency firm in London could adequately exploit the Scottish market unless it can prove it has substantial branch offices in Glasgow or Edinburgh.

It might be permissible to quote here a little story which has served well on previous occasions. It is the one about the Liverpool firm which telexed its agent in Vancouver to meet the managing director on his arrival in Halifax, Nova Scotia. The agent telexed back: "You meet him—you're nearer."

If research has shown that the whole of the Canadian market is potentially valuable, it would be a pity to waste about five-sixths of it by being satisfied with a single agent in Toronto or Montreal.

When appointing agents to a realistic territory, exporters should try to avoid being too influenced by any preconceived ideas based on political or geographical or import tariff considerations. Groupings such as EFTA or EEC (Common Market) or LAFTA or even Benelux really have very little effect upon the way an agent can work. They only play a part when it is a question of setting up a branch factory to supply more than one market from the other side of the customs fence. The only yardstick against which to measure an agent's territory is his proven ability to maintain a satisfactory sales pressure over the whole of it, in terms of the number of times per annum his salesmen can call on the clients in that area, the speed with which he can deliver any necessary spares, the convenience of his local servicing or stocking facilities and the degree to which his promotional resources can penetrate the market in depth.

Naturally, the exporter is faced with the problem of his own capacity to pay sufficiently regular visits to all his agents if they are many and far-flung. Can he afford to service so many regional agents? The answer here is to serve groups of agents in geographically convenient sets of countries with factory representatives. (See page 25.)

It is the factory representative who can think in terms of a

136

political, geographical, or customs unity, because it is his job to supervise general administration, to site central depots, to select main importation channels—all matters which are governed by non-sales factors such as the port facilities, regularity of ship arrivals, air services for urgent parts, comparative tariff structures, and ease of transport between regions or countries.

THE LOCATION OF FACTORY REPRESENTATIVES AND AGENTS IN FOURTEEN MARKET GROUPS

Looking at exports on a global scale, the following fourteen groups suggest themselves as units which can be conveniently supervised by a locally resident factory representative:

1   Northern EEC countries
2   Northern EFTA countries
3   Comecon (probably resident in near-by Western state)
4   North Mediterranean
5   Arab states
6   West Africa
7   East Africa
8   Southern and Central Africa
9   Indian sub-continent
10 South-East Asia
11 Australia—New Zealand
12 North America
13 Central America and Caribbean
14 South America

A senior salesman, with some organising ability, could soon become an expert on his group of markets, making him very competent to appoint new agents or replace those found inadequate, stimulate each one's sales efforts and solve problems with an on-the-spot knowledge of market detail. He could report back fairly frequently to head office, briefing the company management at home and also updating his own knowledge of his firm's developments. He could give intelligent and comprehensive appraisals of future potential in his area and, if senior enough, influence company plans at an early enough stage to make new designs suitable for his territory. Here are some brief notes on the major markets within the groups:

1 NORTHERN EEC COUNTRIES

West Germany, France, Belgium, Netherlands, and Luxembourg are five of the six members of the European Economic Community, or Common Market. The missing one is Italy, which could be included in this group or conveniently placed in the North Mediterranean group, depending upon the scope of the exporting manufacturer's activities.

Internal tariffs have been abolished between the countries and external tariffs are uniform. There is, however, no other unifying factor. The factory representative would have to have a knowledge of French and German and, if possible, Dutch or Flemish, although English is widely known amongst Dutch businessmen.

It is very unlikely that any single agent would be able to handle more than one market satisfactorily, with the possible exception of a Belgian taking in Luxembourg as an extra.

The Netherlands. Only Holland can be taken as a unified territory within the group. It is usually found far more efficient to have more than one agent to develop each of the other countries.

Belgium is split into two linguistic sectors, Walloons and Flemish, and really requires a separate agent to handle each, for there is a great divergency of taste and attitude as well as actual hostility between them. It is probably preferable to have the Dutch agent serve Flemish clients than leave this to a French-speaking Belgian!

France is a country with very regionalised tastes and attitudes. Paris and the surrounding northern area can be one agent's territory, but it would be most efficient to cover the rest of the country with more local agencies. The main centres of operation might be Strasbourg, Lyons, and Marseilles. In addition to the National Federation of Commercial Agents (see Appendix 5) whose members are independent commission agents, France has a highly organised force of about 100 000 travelling salesmen, most of whom are members of the Chambre Syndicale Nationale de la Représentation Commerciale. They can work on a salary or salary plus commission arrangement, for one or more manufacturers, and have to be licensed with the police to receive orders on behalf of each of their principals. These individual salesmen can be hired to build up an intensive sales force with men allocated to very restricted territories, but this would then require a well-organised administrative control, with branch sales offices in a number of strategic cities.

West Germany is by far the most valuable market in the group for most types of product. Although there is linguistic unity in the country, it is still a *Federal* Republic, made up of provinces or *Länder* which have differences of tradition and outlook. There is no centralisation such as that in Paris for France and many German agents keep very much to their own fairly localised territory. There is almost nothing offered as national advertising media, for each major metropolitan area has its own powerful local papers.

Whereas the Ruhr and northern Rhineland used to be a dominating centre of industry, many very fast-growing modern industries have grown up in other areas. Stuttgart is a major automobile production area and is also the site of large-scale electrical manufacture; Munich has a concentration of heavy industry as well as its breweries. In many instances famous factories which were taken over by the state in East Germany (German Democratic Republic) have been re-founded in different areas of West Germany and, in addition, a number of West Berlin firms have found it wise to set up branch industries well away in the Federal Republic. Industry has become widely scattered, adding weight to concentrations of population in different areas.

It would probably be advisable either to appoint agents, or at least ensure that a German agent is properly represented by sub-agents or branch offices, in the following locations: (*a*) Hamburg, (*b*) Dusseldorf, (*c*) Frankfurt, (*d*) Stuttgart, and (*e*) Munich.

If the exporter is selling to Federal Ministries, then he might have to consider Bonn as an alternative or additional vital location.

2 NORTHERN EFTA COUNTRIES

The European Free Trade Association (Sweden, Norway, Denmark, Finland [associate member], United Kingdom, Switzerland,

Austria, and Portugal) is in itself nothing like a "market group" from a sales point of view—even less than the EEC.

Although it has abolished most internal tariffs between the member countries, it still permits individual countries to continue their own external tariffs *vis-à-vis* non-member countries.

There is almost no overlapping of any language, except German in Austria and part of Switzerland and a little Swedish in Finland, otherwise there is no linguistic link. The association includes the richest markets (Sweden, Switzerland) and the poorest (Portugal) of Western Europe, the biggest (UK) and some of the smallest (Austria, Finland).

Every country demands the appointment of at least one agent. It is a fallacy to think that there can be a single agent for Scandinavia or that literature need only be in Swedish. It is actually considered an insult in Norway and Denmark, where they would even prefer it in English if not Norwegian and Danish.

Sweden. Again, regional agencies should be considered. Sweden has two main centres of industry and population—centrally around Stockholm and in the southern tip round Malmö. It should be checked that an agent really does cover these, as well as the more isolated northern area, especially along the coast, where there are pockets of industry with a supporting population.

Norway is a small market but with two very different localised areas—Oslo and Bergen. It is quite common for Norwegian firms, not only foreign ones, to set up offices in each city.

The United Kingdom is not only London. In fact, London-based firms do tend to concentrate only on the Home Counties (counties bordering the capital) but this neglects a very valuable series of major markets round Birmingham, Manchester, Liverpool, Leeds and Newcastle in England; Glasgow, Edinburgh, Dundee, Aberdeen in Scotland; Cardiff and Swansea in South Wales and the North Wales holiday areas; and the metropolitan area of Belfast in Northern Ireland (Ulster). It is also rare to find an agency in England which can cater for the market in Southern Ireland, the Republic of Eire, which is best served from Dublin.

No agent should be appointed with exclusive rights for the whole of the British Isles unless the most stringent checks have been made to confirm his ability (and practice) to carry out real sales efforts in all the areas mentioned above.

Switzerland is a confederation of cantons, each jealous of its great measure of independence. These cantons fall into three main linguistic groups, German-, French- and Italian-speaking, and their populations reflect very closely the habits and tastes of their neighbours over the respective frontiers. The industries also differ in character, with a great deal of heavy engineering in the German areas and light industry, including watchmaking, in the French parts. The German-speaking Swiss tend to understand French, but not vice-versa. It could be a wise precaution to consider two agents, one in, say, Basel or Zürich and another in, perhaps, Geneva or Lausanne.

Austria is a comparatively small market which should be manageable through one agent in Vienna. However, Vienna is in the extreme eastern part of the country and a fairly long and tortuous way from the region bordering Switzerland, Italy, and Germany. Depending upon the value of these western regions, it might be advantageous to select a second agent locally. This would certainly be a good move if the Vienna man also watches over Hungary and Czechoslovakia—an increasingly common practice.

(Portugal is also a member but probably better regarded as part of the Mediterranean market group.)

3 COMECON COUNTRIES

These are centrally planned peoples' republics of eastern Europe—USSR, Poland, Eastern Germany, Czechoslovakia, Hungary, Rumania, Bulgaria, and (not Comecon) Yugoslavia. As it is not really possible to have a factory representative residing in these countries, nor is it possible to appoint private sales agents there, a special approach is required. (See Chapter 9, page 115.) Comecon stands for the Council of Mutual Economic Aid and is a kind of Eastern European Common Market.

It is advisable for the exporting firm to have executives with special experience of communist trading techniques to deal with

Comecon markets. They are potentially very valuable but their systems of buying and distribution are very different from those in the west. However, although regarded as a political "bloc" (becoming less so nowadays), they are not a homogeneous market. Each country has its own separate language, traditions, culture, tastes, character, and industries and there is a big difference from one to the other in the standard of living and the stage of industrialisation.

Although not a member of Comecon, Yugoslavia can be included in the market group because of its communist, nationalised form of industry and the degree of independence afforded the state-owned agencies, a model being followed to a certain extent by some of the other countries.

4 NORTH MEDITERRANEAN COUNTRIES

These are Portugal, Spain, Italy, Greece, Turkey, Cyprus and Israel. They have in common their climate and geographical location. A salesman with a flair for languages might well find one of their languages helping him along with the others, although Turkish is out on its own.

They are also countries which have many tastes and industries fashioned by their close connection with the sea and, furthermore, they are generally areas of less-developed economies working hard to catch up in industry with their richer West European friends and neighbours.

Otherwise, again, each country must be served by its own individual agents, sometimes on a regional basis.

Portugal requires at least an agent in Lisbon as well as, very often, a second agent or sub-agent in Oporto, the other major commercial centre. It is disastrous to try to cope with the Portuguese market with an agent situated in Spain. The two do not mix.

Spain is a big country (by European standards) broken into many parochial centres of commerce and industry, cut off from each other by none-too-easy communications. Exporters have found it possible to handle the market through a single agent in Madrid, but if there is a big scope for the product with large numbers of potential clients, then it is more effective to have agents in Madrid, Barcelona, and Bilbao, the cities with the largest populations and most industries. They are about 400 miles apart across difficult country.

Italy has two halves—the prosperous, industrialised north and the primitive, poor south. Rome may be the capital, but Milan is the main business centre and the obvious choice for the first agent. If Italy looks like being a very big market, then Milan and Naples might be the agency sites to make the most of the whole country.

Greece. Because of the numerous islands and the mountainous area not so well served with roads, Greece might also require more than one agent for thorough development. An agent in Athens is essential, being by far the biggest commercial centre, but the north of the country is quite remote and usually only properly covered from Thessaloniki. The island of Crete would need completely separate coverage from Candia, being over 200 miles across the Aegean Sea from Athens.

Turkey is a country with a few separated centres of population. Istanbul should be the main target for most exporters. It is the busiest area for commerce and the most cosmopolitan in outlook. An agent there might be able to prove his worth in other parts of the country with evidence of bona fide sub-agents or offices. If not, then it is worth while tapping the areas round Izmir and, for government contracts, Ankara, the capital, with agents specially appointed for their immediate territories.

Cyprus poses a special problem because of the split between the Greek and Turkish communities. Depending upon the type of product, it is possible to achieve maximum benefit by appointing a Greek agent in Nicosia at the centre of things, or one in a major port area such as Limassol or Famagusta if importation by sea is an important factor in the marketing operation.

Israel can be covered by a single agent from Haifa or Tel-Aviv, as any part of the country can be reached easily by car.

5 ARAB STATES

This is a very wide area which includes many separate countries: Morocco, Algeria, Tunisia, Libya, United Arab Republic, Saudi Arabia, Jordan, Syria, Lebanon, Iraq, and Kuwait. It does not overwhelm those representatives who take on the job of supervising marketing there. Unlike the other countries mentioned so far, each Arab state consists in the main of a very concentrated area around the capital with sparse population and almost no commerce in the provincial areas. The representative, therefore, need only call on one agent in each country and distribution problems are negligible once the goods have been imported into the capital, as only a small proportion will have to be transported further afield.

There is a certain homogeneity in the group of markets, as Arabic is the common language and most face the same problems of development. There are fairly extreme divergences from the point of view of available foreign exchange to purchase imports and it is by no means the biggest countries which would represent the biggest potential. The important factor is oil revenue. Perhaps the richest of the countries are Kuwait, Libya, and Saudi Arabia, comparative to their population, so that luxury goods and equipment for public amenity developments stand a good chance. A fair proportion of goods imported into the Arab states are either bought by government bodies or specified through foreign buying agencies. It is therefore important for the exporter to prepare the ground well at his own end before visiting the markets, to discover the real seat of business. It is especially important to check that any agent appointed is properly registered with the local authorities and of sufficient status to tackle official departmebts at the right level. In Arab states the sales agents also handle the importation of goods on behalf of customers and many act also as stockists and service engineers, as there is a shortage of firms able to carry out these various functions. (See separate country listings in Chapter 8 for notes on agency legislation.)

Morocco can normally be handled by an agent in Casablanca, but the tiny territory of Tangier might well be given an agent of its own because of the special market created by tourists. Its consumption of luxury goods is far above other Arab cities.

Algeria. Only the coastal strip of Algeria is important to the exporter and this can be covered by an agent located in Algiers.

Tunisia. Likewise, Tunisia is a market which has to be covered by an agent in the capital, Tunis, the centre of the commercial, political, and communications networks of the country. It is similar to most Arab states in that only nationals are allowed to act as agents and to negotiate with government departments.

A market of growing value is **Libya**, where oil has been commercially exploited for the first time this decade. The whole of the population of any trading significance lives along the 1000-mile coast, with concentrations round the present twin capitals, 600 miles apart, of Tripoli and Benghazi, whilst, when the Constitution can be amended, a new capital is being founded at Beida. The best way of keeping abreast of the market's expansion is to have a lively agent in Tripoli who has a branch office in Benghazi and who is well-connected enough to move into Beida at the appropriate time. It is necessary to stay close to the Libyan Government ministries, for they will be placing the biggest foreign orders and only Libyan citizens are permitted to act as agents.

UAR. Agency legislation (see page 114) is of prime importance in the United Arab Republic, for only state-controlled firms are allowed to act as importers or sole agents. Furthermore, many Government tenders have to be negotiated through approved local agents and there are stringent regulations concerning the marking of imported goods in Arabic, which is best left to local people.

As the UAR Government is obviously controlling almost all foreign purchases, whether directly or through nationalised commercial undertakings, the exporter should aim at obtaining the services of a high-ranking agency with the best possible contacts in Cairo.

Exporters interested in **Saudi Arabia** might select the agency location according to the potential type of market. One possible location is Jedda, the main commercial centre and port of entry into the country. On the other hand, Riyadh is the capital and the most modern town, housing the Government ministries, so it is perhaps the best place for negotiating orders for official projects. The Damman area on the Persian Gulf is the site of the country's important oil wells and a valuable location for an agent handling goods for industrial application. It is advisable to have an agent at each of the three places if the market is to be covered thoroughly.

Jordan, Syrian Arab Republic, Lebanon, Iraq, and Kuwait. Though very different markets in character and type of control, each can be adequately covered from their capital cities of Amman, Damascus, Beirut, Baghdad, and Kuwait. In the past, Western firms used to settle for a single agent in a convenient and comfortable spot, such as Beirut, to handle all the neighbouring markets, but nowadays this is not possible, due to fluctuating political differences and the legislation enacted in almost every one of the states decreeing that only their own citizens can act as commercial agents. The good agents can be very good, for many family concerns have a tradition of reliable importation and distribution, but because of their shortage it might be necessary to allow your goods to be sold alongside competitive products. It is sometimes impossible to locate agents with enough know-how to handle technical products. The answer, for many exporters, has been to offer to train some local personnel back in the parent factories.

6 WEST AFRICA

Exporters might be forgiven for not even knowing of the existence of some of the new African states, not to mention the teeming complications of marketing in them. The main ones to be considered are: Nigeria, Ghana, Sierra Leone, Guinea, Senegal, Mali, Gambia, Ivory Coast, Mauritania, Niger, Chad, Gabon, Togoland, and Dahomey.

Either one appoints agents in the biggest markets in West Africa, Nigeria, and Ghana, and controls these from head office with regular personal visits, or one sets up a factory representative with his own office. He will then be the expert who can unravel the various trading knots and see to it that only the minimum of tangle is allowed to develop as new problems arise.

In every facet of life—economics, politics, national identity, education—the West African scene is in a state of change. It is no longer possible to sell to the area through any single agent, nor is it possible to achieve business throughout the territory from afar.

146

It requires on-the-spot supervision by a reliable local agent.

The next few years will continue to be a transitional period, with much of the business in expatriate hands, imports and exports going through French, British, even Lebanese, traders, whilst an increasing amount will be channelled off into state-owned enterprises as the new governments strive to "Africanise" their economies.

Lagos in Nigeria and Accra in Ghana are the obvious commercial centre points for foreign companies in West Africa, but every single one of the countries requires special treatment by a local agent in the capitals if their markets are to be tapped. In a country such as Guinea, many essential imports are the monopoly of the state, which has taken the right to deal direct with foreign suppliers to avoid local agency commission. In others, the major state orders are still placed through buying agents in European capitals—notably London and Paris according to their former British or French dependence. Where local agents are a trading force, they are frequently offices of the big merchant houses which have their own buying and confirming departments in Britain, France, Portugal, Holland, etc.

It is therefore essential for the would-be exporter to West Africa to do a considerable amount of homework through his government trade officers and chamber of commerce and the banks to discover which buying procedure is applicable to his line of goods. Then, if an agent or distributor is found to be desirable or obligatory, the problem is to work hard to persuade a suitable firm to take on the account. Most existing importing organisations are heavily committed to a wide range of goods and will only take on and "sell" (rather than "stock") something new if there is real evidence of its profitability.

The initial hard sell to a selected agent can really only be achieved through a visit to the country concerned after the maximum research has been done at home.

Nigeria is in itself a big enough market to warrant more than one agent, especially as it is a federation of separate territories. At the time of writing the country is torn by civil war, emphasising the non-existence of any unified feeling in the state as a whole. The regions have a great deal of autonomy in carrying out large-scale projects and prefer to negotiate with agents in their own territory, not always with representatives from Lagos.

147

7 EAST AFRICA

To date Kenya, Tanzania, Uganda, Zambia, Malawi, and Ethiopia have made steady progress in their modernisation of their economies. "Africanisation" has not been disrupting their international trade flow. It has, however, to be taken very much into account. So much of local business was previously in the hands of families from India and from the Arab territories that pressure has been brought to bear, especially on expatriates in Kenya, to shift control to local citizens. It is therefore advisable, in the newer states, to check that the potential agent has a secure future in prevailing conditions.

In all the listed countries except Ethiopia local legislation and business methods follow a British pattern.

Kenya, Uganda, and Tanzania. It is probably advisable to appoint agents in four main centres—Nairobi and Mombasa, the capital and main port respectively of Kenya; Kampala in Uganda; and Dar es Salaam in Tanzania. There are many experienced agency firms in these centres, but it must also be remembered that they tend to be overwhelmed with large numbers of accounts. Only the very energetic exporter can expect to receive an adequate promotional service for his goods. It is definitely desirable to have a salaried representative, stationed say in Nairobi, who can watch over the firm's interests in East Africa. A possible alternative is to pay a fee to one of the well-established export houses, which have offices throughout the area, to act as business managers. The export house can help to appoint and supervise the agents, using its know-how which it would take many years for an outsider to accumulate.

Ethiopia is a very cosmopolitan market, with trade being handled by British and other merchant houses, Italian, Arab, and Greek importers and retailers.

Here again the major sales effort for the exporter is towards his chosen agent. If he succeeds in persuading a good distributor to accept the account, the exporter must maintain pressure to see that the goods are "marketed' and not just left in the warehouse. It is even necessary to battle for space on the shelves, often alongside

148

competitive goods from many countries of Europe, America, and the East. It is feasible for a factory representative in Nairobi to exert this pressure through regular visits to Addis Ababa.

8 SOUTHERN AND CENTRAL AFRICA

This area contains the Republic of South Africa, Rhodesia, Angola, and Mozambique. It is an unfortunate fact that the exporter has to keep a constant watchful eye on politics in Africa, because the moves and moods play havoc with international trade more than in any other part of the world. The countries suggested for a Southern and Central Africa market group are not only geographically neighbours but also good friends politically. To a great extent, as things stand at the moment, these areas are cut off from their neighbours to the north which are mainly hostile to the régimes. To be able to export to Southern Africa, therefore, it is essential for the representative to travel direct from the home country or to be resident inside the friendly radius, from the member countries' point of view.

Rhodesia. The embargo on trade with Rhodesia has put that market temporarily out of reach for the majority of products, but, talking in principle, an agent in Salisbury is essential and, if his sub-branch arrangements are not adequate, another agent is desirable in Bulawayo. These two centres would cover most government, industrial, and general commercial outlets.

The Republic of South Africa is of course the biggest market, not only in the southern part but also in the whole of the African Continent.

Its industry and commercial organisation are well developed and it is usually possible to locate qualified agents with general marketing know-how or technical expertise for any range of goods. It is a highly competitive market, however, and agents will not suffer lackadaisical principals. Competition is growing from year to year from products being made locally, often under licence or through joint partnerships with foreign manufacturers. For some lines, the best arrangement might be to use a local industrial firm as agent with a view to starting up manufacture if the market shows sufficient promise.

149

If commission agents or local distributors are to be the long-term approach, then the country should be split into marketing regions, each with its own agent.

Likely choices for locations for most types of product would be Johannesburg in the Transvaal, Durban in Natal and Capetown in the Cape Province. There is a distance of 1000 miles between Johannesburg and Capetown, too much of a stretch for a single local agent to cover adequately, unless he has substantial branch offices staffed with regional salesmen. The types of industry and commerce also differ. Johannesburg is a mining and manufacturing centre and also close to the national administration capital, Pretoria; Capetown is the biggest passenger port for entry into South Africa and also for transit en route to the East and a light-industry manufacturing centre for clothing and food; Durban, the third largest city, is the biggest commercial port and the focus for a number of industries allied to chemicals.

Angola and Mozambique. On the west and east coasts of Africa respectively, these are Portuguese provinces, closely tied to the economy and trading methods of Portugal. Both territories require their own agents. Luanda is the most effective location in Angola, but, due to the shortage of adequate agents for the large number of products being imported, it might be easier to find a willing and able firm to represent a new range in Lobito, a port which handles a big proportion of the country's imports. In Mozambique two agencies would be desirable, one in Lourenco Marques, the main port and capital, and another in the port of Beira.

9 INDIAN SUB-CONTINENT

In spite of political differences, India, Pakistan, and Ceylon are a well-defined market group. All have reached similar stages of development, all have big potential growth but current financial problems, all have a British past in common, so that their commercial attitudes have been moulded in a similar manner.

They cover a very large geographical area, but with the well-organised air services, a centrally situated factory representative can make regular visits to the main centres of each country in the group, supervising the work of the local agents.

Agents must be appointed on a regional basis, for, except for Ceylon, the countries could not possibly be fully served by any single firm.

Pakistan. It has to be remembered that Pakistan consists of two very separate halves, with 1000 miles between the East and West provinces. West Pakistan requires an agent in Karachi, the main city and port. However, the present capital is Rawalpindi, way up in the northern hills, where the Government ministries have been moved. The Government and its nationalised industries are likely to be the biggest customers for many exporters, making it essential to ensure adequate representation close to Government quarters.

Dacca is the main commercial centre of East Pakistan, but many new industries are sprouting round Chittagong which deserves special attention.

Pakistan used to be served, before partition, by the old established merchant houses in India. Since gaining independence the country has had to build a new trade structure and many new firms staffed by energetic young executives have been founded, taking on agencies for products badly needed by the country. These new organisations respond well to active co-operation and training from sympathetic exporters and offer a very suitable way into the market. At the same time there are offices in Pakistan of the very experienced export houses, mainly British, which can give excellent service if they can be convinced of the worthiness of a new line.

India. With its dozen or more semi-independent states and its 300-odd different languages, India is really a political collection of many varied nations. It has to be treated as a motley group of markets, with separate agencies, probably, in Delhi, Bombay, Calcutta, Madras, and possibly even Hyderabad and Bangalore. Every type of agency is practicable—commission agent, sole distributor, stockist, wholesaler-importer. Great influence is wielded by the merchant houses, mostly of British origin, and considerable business is possible through buying agents in London and elsewhere. Special know-how is required in connection with payment of goods bought for India because of the complicated and rigid exchange control. In addition to the hurdles of the customer's preference and the price, there are those of import licence and currency allocation.

Ceylon represents a similar picture, except that it is a much smaller territory. It is usually sufficient to have one good agency in Colombo to serve the whole island. For technical products, it may be necessary to seek out a European agent with a trained staff, but for general consumer goods there are many lively local traders with sufficient importation experience and sales contacts to do good service. There is a strong trend to divert as much business as possible in the future into the hands of Ceylon citizens. This is a point to bear in mind, although it might be some time before the capital plant imports can be entirely handled by non-Europeans.

10 SOUTH-EAST ASIA

Any company representative would have a right to jib at being expected to coax, coddle, and clobber agents in all the territories of this region: Burma, Thailand, Laos, Cambodia, Malaysia, Singapore, Indonesia, the Philippines, Hong Kong, and Japan.

If each one were to be penetrated in depth, then they would probably have to be split into two smaller groups for two supervisors to control. However, in the system of selecting really key markets, it is probable that only a proportion of the South-East Asian countries would show themselves to merit the full treatment —and nothing less than the full treatment is worth while.

Burma is one of the world's underdeveloped countries which is seeking its own way forward with as much emphasis as possible on local participation in business and with the state becoming involved with most major transactions.

For most general types of goods, an agent in Rangoon is enough to cover the whole market, simply because at any distance from the capital the commercial potential is very slight. Most of the country's wealth is in the metropolitan area.

Where big projects are concerned, and this is the aspect with the biggest allocation of foreign currency from the Burmese Government, the state is the sole purchaser and it usually prefers to buy direct to avoid paying commission to its own local citizens. The

Rangoon agent, if properly selected and guided, can be a most useful contact in keeping the exporter informed of prospects for this wider scope of business and can always be rewarded with a fee for consultation work, even if the exporter's factory representative makes the actual contact with the state buying executives.

Thailand has been one of the most stable of the economies in this part of the world and has qualified for a great amount of foreign aid (mainly American), much of which has been invested in constructing roads, power stations, and light-industrial estates.

Bangkok is the only really satisfactory location for an agent and it is difficult to find a suitable firm for anything but a new and exciting product, for there is already a scramble for shelving space on the part of the many would-be exporters from Europe, the USA, Japan, and Australia. Once found, and appointed, a good agent in Thailand has to be regularly visited and encouraged to maintain his interest in the face of the competition knocking on his door.

Introductions to the market can be arranged often through the traditional export houses, via their head offices or branches in Europe—London, Paris, Amsterdam. Banks have particularly good contacts amongst local businessmen and, where financial backing is necessary for marketing the product, their recommendation would be essential.

Laos and Cambodia. Here it is the French-speaking exporter, not the English-speaker, who will feel most at home. The markets are comparatively underdeveloped with primitive methods of distribution. Imports are strictly controlled by licence and currency regulations. One agent in Phnom Penh for Cambodia and one in Luang Prabang for Laos is an adequate arrangement.

Malaysia is an important market in South-East Asia even though it has a small population of about 7 million. An agent is essential in the federal capital Kuala Lumpur, centrally situated on the Malay Peninsula.

Sabah (North Borneo) and Sarawak. If there are potential business outlets for a product there, a separate local representative is needed, but this would pose a few problems as experienced traders are in very short supply.

Singapore, although a small island, houses 2 million people and is a valuable market for many exporters. It is a major South-East Asian port, both for entry and exit of goods and for transit between East and West. It can only be properly served by its own agent.

Indonesia's multiple islands are an exporter's headache. Because of recent unrest and change, many firms are tempted to leave them alone and yet other competitors are seen to be conducting big business there. It is worth doing some desk research and then paying a visit, including calls on local embassies, banks, and merchant houses to see what the future holds. The country is in desperate need of a very wide range of goods and imports a great deal when currency is available. There are signs that more international aid will be forthcoming as confidence grows in its affairs. Long-term credit is an important factor in obtaining big orders.

The market has been served through merchants who import, export, retail, wholesale, act on commission—handling any and every side according to business opportunity. The major purchases, however, especially of capital plant, now stem from Government sources.

The best solution is to appoint an agent in Djakarta who has adequate contacts throughout the island of Java and on the other less populated islands. At the same time it is essential to check that he has the right status for access to the state's nationalised trading corporations and practical experience in obtaining the import and exchange licences for the goods in question.

The Philippines. Whereas Indonesia has special trading ties with the communist countries which supplied much of its needs, The Philippines have had the closest trade connections with USA exporters, so that English has taken over from Spanish as the commercial language of the Philippines' 7000 islands. It is, luckily, not necessary to appoint an agent on each of these! Manila is the centre of the country's main concentration of commerce and industry and the only big port of entry. An agent in Manila is likely to have his own branches for distribution in Cebu and Davao, etc.

Hong Kong is possibly the most intensively commercial spot on the surface of the Earth. Only thirty-five square miles of it, but it crams in every conceivable type of industry—from banking to batteries, ship-repair to spinning cotton. There are hundreds of agencies in the colony—Chinese, British merchants, American joint ventures. Only one agent is needed and he is likely to be active and energetic otherwise he would not have survived. The main thing is servicing him promptly and efficiently.

Hong Kong and Singapore are the two favourite choices for a centre of operations when considering setting up a factory representative in the area. There is great freedom of access and communications are excellent with all parts of the area—with Japan, the Philippines, Malaya, Indonesia, Taiwan, Thailand, Burma, etc.

Japan is the home of those extraordinary, unparalleled giant trading companies (see Chapter 10). If one exports through them, then they will be able to make use of their branches which blanket the whole country. They might also be able to use their branch offices in other parts of South-East Asia for products with big potential.

If the choice is a more conventional commission agent or independent distributor, it is advisable to appoint more than one, or at least to check the single agent's ability to cover the market outside Tokyo. Japan, too, has a very regionalised geography, especially as it is such a long country with highly concentrated pockets of population and industry isolated by mountain ranges or on islands across the water. On the main island, the big markets are Tokyo, Osaka, Nagoya, and Kure or Hiroshima. The islands of Hokkaido in the north and Shikoku and Kyushu in the south could merit separate representation.

11 AUSTRALIA AND NEW ZEALAND

It is usually a good investment to set up a factory representative to control these markets through a series of strategically placed agents. It is probably best to regard the two countries as a group of eight different markets. Naturally, they have many things in common. These are the English language, highly developed commercial and industrial structures, rapid growth and an insistence on high-quality goods and the best possible servicing arrangements.

It is usually a frustrating business for both sides if a manufacturer, situated remotely in Europe or the USA, tries to cope with agents without the assistance of some authoritative intermediary, such as a salaried factory representative. It is rare for a distant manufacturer to be able to give the detailed attention and quick decisions which the markets demand for proper exploitation.

The eight markets and agency locations might be:

1	New South Wales and Canberra	Sydney
2	Victoria	Melbourne
3	Queensland	Brisbane
4	South Australia	Adelaide
5	Western Australia	Perth
6	Tasmania	Hobart
7	New Zealand, North Island	Auckland or Wellington
8	New Zealand, South Island	Christchurch or Dunedin

In Australia vast developments are taking place right across the 2600 miles breadth of the country, many of them being projects financed by the highly independent states. The only way to keep in touch with them is through an active, mobile agent in each state and even then he is going to have his hands full, for these regional territories are vast.

New Zealand has special problems because of the present import licensing system, which issues permits to import based on previous levels of business handled by the agent in that particular line of goods. It can make it very difficult to change an agent, for the previous one would retain the import rights and a new one, if operating on a smaller scale or if a newcomer to that range of goods, might have difficulty in obtaining licences equal to the level of turnover he could achieve.

The markets cry out for the personal touch, so that no opportunities are missed and to avoid errors which could lose a manufacturer a lot of ground. When one exporter slips, there are many others, from the USA, Europe, and Japan, to make the most of the situation.

12 NORTH AMERICA

Two countries only—United States of America and Canada—but they represent a vast market group in size and value.

It is not practicable to handle either country with only one agent. There is very little centralisation of population, finance or industry, so that only a small proportion of potential business can be tapped from any one big city.

The most successful exporters to the USA and Canada have treated the markets with the respect they deserve and set up branch factories and fully fledged sales operations, competing on level terms with local suppliers. However, this is not practicable for every product or manufacturer, nor is it always advisable as an initial entrée. Where agents are to be employed, it is best to regard the countries as a collection of many different markets. Probably the smallest number of regional divisions ought to be four in Canada and five in the USA.

For the USA these might be:

1   New York, serving the Atlantic seaboard
2   Chicago, for states such as Illinois, Ohio, Michigan, Indiana
3   San Francisco, covering California, Nevada, Arizona, Utah
4   Seattle, with responsibility for the north-west
5   New Orleans, taking in as much of the south-east as possible

For Canada:

1   Montreal, for Quebec and the Atlantic Provinces
2   Toronto for the immediate industrial area and Ontario
3   Winnipeg for the mid-western provinces of Manitoba, Saskatchewan, and Alberta
4   Vancouver, covering the western coast and British Columbia

All the states in the USA and the provinces of Canada, in addition to having regional promotional media, differences in types of

157

industry or commerce and varying climatic conditions, also boast substantial official budgets for major local development projects. It takes a local agent to have the know-how and contacts to make the most of every opportunity.

There have been examples of European firms with a single agent in the USA (mostly New York) being responsible for not only Canada and the USA but also Mexico. These firms have actually been satisfied with results until they were urged to analyse them. They invariably found that although turnover was high, it stemmed almost exclusively from the east coast of the USA, so that over 95 per cent of the North American market was totally neglected.

In the same way there are examples of Australian firms being satisfied with business from an agent in San Francisco or Los Angeles, the first cities you arrive at if you fly from Sydney. Only rarely did they obtain orders for delivery to Chicago or Miami or New Orleans. The most they could expect was an occasional visit by the agent to New York.

One way in which a British exporter safeguarded his own interests whilst giving full opportunities to his agents in the USA, was to allocate to four agents about one quarter each of the whole country. He then set targets to be achieved in different sectors of their territories. If these were not achieved, he had the right to deprive them of the sales rights in that sector, where he would appoint a separate agent to cover it specifically. The USA became that exporter's biggest market, bigger even than the UK home market.

If the countries are to be intensively penetrated, it is advisable to bear additional agency locations in mind, including for the USA: Miami, Washington, Detroit, St Louis, St Paul, Dallas, Denver, and Salt Lake City; and for Canada: Halifax, Ottawa, Regina, Edmonton, or Calgary.

Making the most of these markets means setting up eventually a central sales office staffed by salaried executives who can give the immediate service required by North American agents. It is only from a base on the continent itself that sufficiently regular visits can be made to each region. For a visiting salesman from Europe, it would require at least two months' intensive touring to give local agents just a few days each to solve problems and meet important clients. At the end of that time the visitor would be feeling somewhat exhausted and not too competent to think quickly and make intelligent decisions, especially if his knowledge of local trends were sketchy. If there is no resident representative to cover the markets, then one alternative might be to send out a number of executives from head office to concentrate on a smaller section, going more frequently for shorter periods.

It must also be remembered how much spadework might be done back in Europe with the buying offices representing North American department stores, fashion houses, and supermarkets. (See pages 32–5.)

13 CENTRAL AMERICA AND CARIBBEAN MARKET GROUP

This would be a very stimulating mixed bag of markets for a regular factory representative; it comprises: Mexico, Guatemala, Salvador, Belize (British Honduras), Honduras, Nicaragua, Costa Rica, Panama, West Indies, Haiti, Dominican Republic, and the Bahamas. It embraces countries which speak English, Spanish, and French, the one big area of Mexico and the dozens of smaller territories.

It requires a specialist to appreciate the different potentials of each market and the ins and outs of the very varying import regulations.

Most of these countries have local laws restricting the trading activities of non-citizens. Some are members of local customs unions, but each is still very independently minded, striving to preserve its own national identity and avoid being swallowed up by giant foreign companies. On the other hand, participation in local manufacture is greatly encouraged, so long as control is kept in local hands.

European exporters need to install a factory representative to look after their interests because of the dominating influence of American and Canadian exporters who compete very keenly on delivery and speedy service.

No agent in one country can realistically be expected to handle a neighbouring market, but a single agent in each country is sufficient, even in Mexico, where the area in a 250-mile radius round Mexico City takes in the main towns of Guadalajara and Veracruz and the prosperous holiday region of Acapulco.

If the exporter is hoping to market luxury goods, then the number of markets in this group would be cut down to a very few, for most of the countries are doing their utmost to preserve foreign exchange for only essential goods and production equipment. The holiday area of the Bahamas and the free port of Panama are outlets for high-quality consumer goods, otherwise the main openings are for capital plant and partnerships in the local production of consumer durables.

14 SOUTH AMERICA

Most of the remarks made in the previous section apply also to this enormous group of markets: Venezuela, Guyana, Colombia, Ecuador, Brazil, Peru, Bolivia, Paraguay, Uruguay, Chile, and Argentina. It is unlikely that an exporter of luxury goods or non-essential products would find it worth while appointing a factory representative, for it might be that only a couple of countries, say Venezuela and Uruguay, would be of special interest.

If, however, it is a matter of selling equipment or industrial materials, then there is big potential in each of these countries and it would take a specialist on the spot to nurse the area as a whole. Factory representatives have been set up by European firms in Rio de Janeiro or Buenos Aires, whilst North Americans have chosen Caracas, and Japanese and Australian firms have frequently located an office in Lima or Santiago. It has depended upon the easiest means of communication with head office, the comparative cost of living and on the ability of the executives to speak Spanish or Portuguese (Brazil is the Portuguese-speaking country).

Although some of the countries are very big in area (Brazil is as big as Australia; Argentina and Chile are both three times longer than the British Isles), they are very underdeveloped, so that small pockets round the one or two chief towns account for the biggest part of the country's population and commercial activity.

The whole of South America, therefore, can be adequately covered by a total of eleven agents, one in each capital city except in Brazil, where for the moment Rio de Janeiro would be more valuable than the newly-founded capital of Brasilia.

Because of the severe competition for the generally limited number of good agents in each line of business in South America, it is advisable to allow the factory representative fairly wide-ranging authority to make decisions. In this way he can authorise agents to take certain steps to gain orders without long delays and explanations arising from constant reference back to head office. In the latter case, the agent would soon get tired of losing business and commission. He could then easily be persuaded to change to a more dynamic principal.

It is good practice, and very common too, for North American firms to have their own representatives resident in South America to keep a very close watch on developments. They can obtain the "feel" of the market, develop good working relations with the various agents, and can solve problems with immediate reference to the client. It is even more necessary for more distant principals to keep someone on the spot.

Glossary of Export Terms

Acceptance Credit. An arrangement whereby the buyer in the export market pays his bank for goods after a specified period counted from the time when he has seen and approved delivery. The exporter is able to discount the bill of exchange immediately or alternatively wait for payment on the specified day, when he will receive the amount in full.

Bill of Exchange. Document which covers payment for goods and which specifies the date for payment to be made, the currency in which payment is to be calculated and which party is to meet bank charges or interest charges. A Bill is drawn by the exporter and presented to the foreign purchaser through a bank. (See examples, page 173.)

Bill of Lading. Document which, when completed and signed, specifies the person or firm authorised to collect goods being shipped. It describes the goods, gives the details of the ship on which they have been loaded, states the destination and the condition in which they were loaded and shows whether or not freightage has been paid. It is issued by the shipping firm.

Brussels Nomenclature. Sometimes referred to as BTN (Brussels Tariff Nomenclature), but officially it is Nomenclature for the Classification of Goods in Customs Tariffs. About 100 countries are signatories to the Brussels Convention on Nomenclature, a committee set up by the Customs Co-operation Council which is located in Brussels. It classifies goods by sectors, chapters, and headings, with rules of interpretation, so that exporters in different countries can ascertain in advance how their own goods will be classified and what tariffs they will be subject to. It also provides a standardised means of comparison for export and import statistics of different countries.

Buying Office. An office set up in a foreign country for the purpose of locating suppliers of required goods. It can either be a subsidiary of a single importer or it can act on behalf of a number of different non-competitive principals. Definition often overlaps with terms "buying house" and "buying agent." (See pages 32–3.)

Case of Need. A local agent authorised to assume certain responsibilities on behalf of the distant exporter in the event of non-payment by a customer after the goods have been landed. The local bank handling the transaction can deal with the "case of need" up to the limits specified by the exporter giving the authorisation.

Certificate of Origin (or of value, or of quality). These certificates can be requested by the importer or, very frequently, by the customs authorities of the buyer's country. The certificate of origin is essential where, for example, there are favourable duty terms for goods from specific countries. The intention is to prevent goods being shipped conveniently through third markets to qualify illegally for lower tariffs. The certificates may be issued by various authorities, according to the requirement, sometimes signed by the local consul of the buyer's country, by the exporting customs, by a chamber of commerce or, for quality, by a recognised technical or research institute which verifies certain tests.

C.i.f. The abbreviation stands for "cost, insurance, freight" and means that a quotation includes all costs up to the point of the goods reaching the named port of arrival. However, the purchaser is in fact responsible for them after they have been accepted by the shipping firm. The buyer pays landing expenses, import taxes and other charges on arrival. He receives the necessary documents so that he can claim damages where necessary. Other variations of the term can be c.i.f. and c., which is cost, insurance, freight and commission (stated as a specific percentage) and shows that the price includes the agent's commission.

C.i.f. duty paid would include all costs up to the goods arriving at the port of entry specified and also any tariff charges, but the importer would still have to meet any other local taxes, such as purchase tax or added value tax.

C.i.f. Delivered Agent's Go-Down Duty Paid. This term makes it clear that all charges are met in advance by the exporter, delivering the goods straight to the agent's own warehouse inland. It is a form of quotation more common as more goods are trans-shipped in containers, or on roll-on/roll-off lorries on ferries, or specialised aircraft.

Concessionnaire. A firm given the right to handle principal's goods on a given market, normally a sole concessionnaire who has the exclusive right to a specific territory or group of clients.

Confirming House. Acts on behalf of the foreign buyer. Can negotiate a price with the local exporter and pays promptly as soon as goods are shipped, making arrangements with the buyer for payment on agreed credit terms. Can be treated as a home market customer by the exporter, as the confirming house takes responsibility for shipment to the foreign client and pays in local currency. (See page 35.)

Consignment Stock. Goods delivered to an agent for him to sell them on behalf of the principal. They remain the property of the principal and any monies collected for their sale also remain the property of the principal, the agent receiving a commission as remuneration for his sales efforts. It is essential to make the status of consignment absolutely clear in a contract (see page 21) otherwise, for example, in the event of the agent's bankruptcy, his creditors could take possession of the goods or the cash received from sales.

Consular Invoice. This is a specific form of authenticated invoice required by some countries before goods can be imported. It confirms for the foreign authorities the value of the goods being shipped for the purpose of assessment of duty and other taxes. It is especially necessary in those countries which demand that agents lodge the full amount of cash for pre-payment of imported goods as a means of discouraging imports.

D/A: Documents Against Acceptance. Instead of sending documents directly to the purchaser, they are sent via a bank with an accompanying bill of exchange. The documents are handed over to the purchaser by the bank when he has signed his acceptance of the bill.

***Del Credere* Risk.** Financial responsibility—suffering any loss resulting from default in payment by the purchaser.

Demurrage Charges. Any additional expenses caused by delay in collection of goods. For example, if customer defaults and does not collect goods from a port or airport warehouse, someone has to pay the storage fees. A "case in need" can be given authority in advance to collect goods in these circumstances and claim the charges from the exporter to avoid further delay and expense.

Distributor. The type of agent who purchases the goods on his own account to sell at a profit. A sole distributor obtains certain concessions from the principal on exclusive territory and special discounts in return for services—not handling competitive goods, maintaining certain targets, etc. (See page 28.)

Documentary Bill. A bill of exchange accompanied by the title documents which are only handed to the purchaser, giving him the right to collect the goods, when he has accepted the conditions stated on the bill.

Document of Title. Document such as a fully signed and completed bill of lading which gives the recipient the right to take possession of goods.

D/P: Documents Against Payment. As D/A except that the documents are handed over when the bill of exchange is actually paid, not simply accepted.

Drawn at Sight. When a bill of exchange is drawn at sight it means that the importer has to meet the payment immediately without days of grace after delivery of the goods.

Exchange Control. Regulations made by either the importer's country or the exporter's country governing the receipt or payment of home or foreign currency. For the buyer it often means that foreign exchange is limited and only allowed to be used for certain specified types of goods or when a special allocation has been allowed. For the exporter it implies usually that there is a limitation on the length of credit which can be offered, payment for exported goods having to be received within a set period of time. Payment must be received in a currency conforming to the regulations, usually one freely convertible.

Export House. A comprehensive term describing the modern version of the export merchant who might act as confirming house, factor, buying office, merchant shipper or any combination. (See page 26.)

Export Licences. Permits required for the export of certain restricted ranges of goods. These might include military material which is embargoed for many markets, or fine art works which a country wishes to retain as far as possible, or certain raw materials which are in short supply and vital to a country's own economy.

Export Merchant. See "Export house" and page 27.

Factors. They act on behalf of the exporter and pay him for his goods immediately on dispatch, taking on responsibility for collection of payment or affording credit terms to the buyer overseas. Remuneration is a fee in proportion to value involved and risk undertaken. (See page 36.)

Factory Representative. Salaried employee based abroad to watch over the marketing arrangements in a specific group of markets. He normally supervises the local agents' operations on behalf of his company. (See page 25 and Chapter 11.)

Free Alongside Ship. F.a.s. (followed by name of port or name of ship) is a quotation which includes costs of transport to that point but which does not meet the costs of loading the goods on board, nor does it include any shipping or insurance charges for the onward journey.

Free on Board. F.o.b. quotations include the cost of delivering the goods on to a ship at a named port of embarkation, but leave it to the purchaser or importer to meet the actual freight and insurance charges and all duties and taxes at the other end. It is usually a better service for the foreign buyer if the exporter quotes c.i.f. or even further and these quotations are often encouraged by the exporter's own country, for it means greater foreign currency earnings. However, for the same reasons, many importing countries insist on f.o.b. prices for they can frequently pay the additional expenses to their own shipping lines without paying out valuable foreign exchange. Quotations, as far as possible, should be formed to suit the convenience of the agent and the customer, adding to the sales effort.

Force Majeure. Circumstances outside the control of either party to a contract preventing them, through no fault or negligence on their side, from carrying out the agreement. A force majeure clause avoids penalties being imposed for such things as late delivery when the supplier is quite unable to meet a date due to unforeseeable and unavoidable circumstances.

Forward Exchange. The sale of foreign currency arranged for a fixed date in the future but agreeing a rate of exchange which will not alter regardless of any fluctuations in the interim period. If an exporter ships goods quoted in a foreign currency to be paid at a future date, he could incur a serious loss if the foreign currency has lost value by the time payment is made. It is possible to cater for this in advance by contracting with a bank to sell the currency when it arrives at an agreed price.

Free of Particular Average. F.p.a. is an insurance term. It describes the kind of policy which only covers damage to the whole shipment and not a portion of it. It is commonly used for shipments of single items of equipment, which, unlike numbers of separate packages, can hardly be lost or pilfered piecemeal.

Frozen Debt. The halting of any payment transaction if a complaint has been raised which implies that the terms of a contract have not been met. If frozen officially, it can avoid claims for additional interest, for example.

167

Indents. Orders placed by export house or buying office for goods specified by their principals.

Irrevocable Credit. This is a guarantee in advance that payment for goods will be made at a specified time or when certain conditions have been met. The irrevocable credit is issued by a bank (home or overseas) and only the exporter who is to receive the payment can agree to its withdrawal.

Manufacturer's Agent. Person or firm acting on behalf of a manufacturer. It is one attempt at standardisation of terminology and is usually taken to indicate an agent working on a commission basis. Half of this book is an attempt to define the word "agent" which is very loosely used meaning some form of representation, especially in a foreign market.

Merchant. A person or firm buying goods as a principal on his own account and reselling at a profit. He may or may not, according to agreement, handle competitive lines. If he takes on additional responsibilities of promotion in return for exclusive rights, he is probably described as a "distributor."

On Consignment. See "Consignment stock." Shipments "on consignment" remain the property of the exporter until purchased by the agent's customer.

Open Cover. Another insurance term, describing a very convenient policy for regular exporters. It automatically, for a twelve months' period, insures all shipments, the details being advised and recorded retrospectively and the premiums paid at specified intervals for the foregoing period according to the sums which have been at risk.

Performance Guarantee. A kind of deposit paid to a bank by an exporter who has been awarded a contract by tender. Foreign governments and public authorities safeguard themselves by demanding a performance guarantee to cover wasted expenditure if the winner of the contract cannot meet his responsibilities.

Resident Salesman. A salaried employee in an overseas market as distinct from a salesman working on commission or for an agent. His insurance, holidays, pensions, and so on, are the responsibility of the exporter.

Revocable Credit. A promise to pay which can be revoked by the customer, leaving the supplier with no guarantee. It is often acceptable when the buyer is a customer of long-standing whose reliability is beyond question by the exporter. It is more than a mere letter of contract, because it is issued by a bank and will produce payment automatically on the due date unless the buyer actually withdraws it.

Right of Redress. A legal justification to take action against a party who has not fulfilled the terms of a contract.

Salaried Representative. The status of a salesman in a foreign market taken on by an exporter who pays a regular salary and meets his sales expenses. The principal becomes responsible for the welfare, insurance, and so on, of the salesman, although this can be on a proportional basis if the salesman is, by common agreement, also working on behalf of other principals.

Scheduled Territories. Those countries designated as the Sterling Area where transactions can be in sterling without the restriction of British exchange control.

Shipping Agent. Firm which organises the shipment of goods to foreign markets, taking over the necessary documentation, selection and booking of transport, correct packing, custom's procedures and insurance on behalf of the exporter.

Status Report. A report on the financial standing of a firm or individual made by a bank, or, when made by a commercial office, a report on the reputation and business ability of an individual or agent. (See sample bank reports, pages 171–2.)

Sterling Area. See "Scheduled Territories."

Stockist. See definition on page 28. A stockist purchases goods from an exporter or from his sole distributor and guarantees to maintain a certain level of stocks.

Tender Guarantee. A deposit, equal to a specified percentage of the quotation, placed in a bank by manufacturers participating in a tender. It can also, in fact, be a guarantee issued by the manufacturer's bankers, the purpose being to ensure the seriousness and the financial standing of those competing for government or public body business.

T.V.A. *Taxe sur la valeur ajoutée* (tax on added value) is imposed on all goods manufactured in or entering France. Being an internal tax, it is quite separate from import tariffs. It is payable by whoever is responsible for the customs clearance of imported goods, either the buyer (if it is c.i.f.) or by the exporter if he has quoted all-in price for delivery to the customer.

Usance Bill. A bill of exchange drawn so that payment is not due until a specified period (perhaps thirty or sixty days after signature by the customer) has passed since the bill and the shipping documents were presented by a bank.

With Recourse. A finance house, for example, can undertake to obtain payment for goods from the foreign customer with or without recourse to the manufacturer, meaning that the loss, if the customer defaults, is to be borne by the manufacturer (with recourse) or by the finance house (without recourse). The fee for handling the transaction will vary according to the nature of the risk undertaken.

With Particular Average. When an insurance policy is taken w.p.a. it means that it covers damage to the whole or to any part of the shipment in proportion to the total value.

Specimen Status Reports

Examples of the sort of reports on agents provided by a well-known international bank. Names, of course, are fictitious.

SPECIMEN 1

X Y Z Company, Commercial Esplanade, Cosmos City, Republic of South Vania.
Registered 5 April 1960
Authorised capital: £100 000
Issued and paid: £80 000
Directors: J Sellers, B Q Warrits and I Stockem. A highly respectable directorate and a most satisfactory account maintained since 1960. May be considered perfectly good for their normal business engagements.

SPECIMEN 2

Whee Reps Inc, Main Avenue, Port Town, Girania.
Company registered 5 June 1961
Authorised capital: $US 250 000
Issued and paid: $US 200 000
Directors: A M Brown, E S Black, K L Green. Respectable directorate and a satisfactory account maintained since 1961. We do not feel they would enter into any commitment they could not see their way to fulfil.

SPECIMEN 3

The Orl Wright Agency Co Ltd, Tonhamp, Strinia.
Company registered 18 September 1965
Authorised capital: £90 000
Issued and paid: £65 000
Directors: C Dee, E Eff, G Hahn and L Emms. Directors ar respectable but the Company's resources appear to be fully committed at present. We suggest dealings are only undertaken on a fully secured basis.

Specimen Bills of Exchange

EXCHANGE FOR £412 - 3 - 6   London, 26th September 1968

At sight .... pay this sole Bill of Exchange to the Order of

ourselves

Four hundred and twelve pounds 3/6 d.

Payable at the current rate of exchange for sight drafts on London

Value received   which place to Account

To Weisswurst A.G.   For B. Brown and Sons,

Hamburg, W. Germany   J. Hope, Director

Foreign B/X. Printed & Sold by Waterlow & Sons Ltd, London, E.C.2.

1 STERLING DRAFT PAYABLE AT SIGHT

The drawees (the German firm paying the bill) bear the
exchange charges.

EXCHANGE FOR US $ 195 00   London, 26th September 1968

At 60 days sight (second unpaid) pay this first Bill of Exchange to the Order of

ourselves

One hundred and ninety five United States dollars

Payable at the current rate of exchange for sight drafts on New York

Value received   which place to Account

To Samarianas & Cia.,   per pro Bobble Smelters Ltd.,

Santiago, Chile   Frederick Little, Secretary

Foreign B/X. Printed & Sold by Waterlow & Sons Ltd., London, E.C.2.

2 CURRENCY DRAFT PAYABLE 60 DAYS AFTER ACCEPTANCE

The drawees (the Chilean firm receiving the goods) bear the
exchange charges. They "accept" the bill by signing it when it is
presented by the bank.

Code of Ethics for Manufacturers' Agents

The following is the code of ethics for agents as expounded by The Manufacturers' Agents' Association of Great Britain and Ireland (Incorporated).

1   To be Accorded the Manufacturer by the Manufacturer's Agent

(*a*) Comply with the established policies of the manufacturer;

(*b*) Conscientiously cover the territory assigned;

(*c*) Avoid misrepresentation in any form or manner;

(*d*) Restrict lines or accounts with principals to those that can be well handled; and,

(*e*) Give the manufacturer the same loyal service as the Agent operating his own business, expects from his own employees.

2   To be Accorded the Manufacturer's Agent by the Manufacturer

(*a*) Enter into a fair and clearly worded agreement with the Manufacturer's Agent;

(*b*) Make the agreement cancellable by either party during its first year on suitable advance written notice, but subsequently only for failure of either party to comply with its terms, or by mutual consent;

(*c*) Refrain from any modification whatever of the terms of such agreement except by mutual consent after full and friendly discussion of the reasons for such desired modification;

(*d*) Extend to the Manufacturer's Agent the same benefits available to the manufacturer's own salaried employees wherever possible;

(*e*) Refrain from absorbing, refusing or cutting the Manufacturer's Agent's established commissions for any reason whatever: and,

(*f*) Provide practical and dignified means for friendly arbitration of all controversial points that may arise, between Agent and principal.

3 To be Accorded one Manufacturer's Agent by another Manufacturer's Agent

(*a*) Exchange trade information in the mutual interest;

(*b*) Avoid any suggestion of agreement to divide commissions with those representing other than the Agent's own principals;

(*c*) Refrain from soliciting from manufacturers the known lines or accounts of other established Manufacturers' Agents by unfair methods; and,

(*d*) Co-operate to upbuild the profession of the Manufacturer's Agent—by joining the Association established for that purpose, subscribing to its aims and objectives, and in every practical way working to advance the interest of all Manufacturers' Agents and self-employed Travellers.

Valuable Address Lists

AGENTS' ASSOCIATIONS

Members of the International Union of Commercial Agents and Brokers, Spui 23–27, Amsterdam

Belgium

Groupe des Chambres Syndicales et Unions Professionelles d'Agents Independants, Courtiers et Concessionnaires du Commerce et de l'Industrie (AICC), 105 Rue Beekman, Bruxelles 18

Britain

The Manufacturers' Agents' Association, PO Box 8, Majestic House, High Street, Staines, Middlesex

France

Federation Nationale des Agents Commerciaux, 23 Rue des Mathurins, Paris 8e

Germany

Centralvereinigung Deutscher Handelsvertreter- und Handelsmakler-Verbände (CDH), Geleniusstrasse 1, Köln-Lindenthal

Israel

Union of Manufacturers Agents and Brokers of Israel, PO Box 2357, 6 Rothschild Blvd, Tel-Aviv

Italy

Federazione Nazionale Associazioni Agenti e Rappresentanti di Commercio, Piazza Belgiojoso 1, Milano

Holland

Het Nederlands Verbond van Tussenpersonen, Spui 23–27, Amsterdam

Scandinavia

The Federation of Nordic Commercial Agents, Meltzersgate 4, Oslo 2. Members of this federation are: The Association of Danish Import Agents

Borsen, Christiansgade, København K/Copenhagen

The Federation of Norwegian Commercial Agents, Meltzersgate 4, Oslo

Finnish Foreign Trade Agents Federation, Kluuvikatu 3, Helsinki 10

The Federation of Swedish Commercial Agents, Narvavägen 27, Stockholm-ö

Switzerland

Verband Schweizerischer Agenten de Lebensmittel-Branche en Gros, Postfach 3243, 8023 Zürich

Verband Kaufmännischer Agenten der Schweiz, Nüschelerstrasse 22/Pelikanstr., Zürich 1

USA

Manufacturers' Agents National Association, 626 North Garfield Avenue, PO Box 991, Alhambra, California

SOME EUROPEAN INDEPENDENT BUYING OFFICES

These represent department stores, speciality stores, importers and manufacturers throughout the world, with special connections in the USA, Canada, Australia, and Japan

Austria

A. A. Braunstein, 24 Wollzeile, Wien/Vienna

Belgium

Detobel & Claes, 3 Rue d'Assaut, Bruxelles

Britain

Dean, Warburg Ltd, 81 New Bond Street, London W1

France

E Boas & Co, 8 Rue Ambroise-Thomas, Paris

Germany

Reimann & Co, 43 Blittersdorfplatz, Frankfurt am Main

Italy

Krieger Ltd, 11 Parioni Str., Firenze/Florence

177

Denmark
Scandinavian Buying Service, Vestersbrogade 15, København/
Copenhagen
Spain
G. Matteini, Matteini Building, Avenida de America Km 5,
Madrid
Switzerland
Siegfried Bollag & Co, 109 Seebahnstrasse, Zurich

OTHER EXPORT ORGANISATIONS IN THE UK

British Agents Register
BAR House, 119 Gunnersbury Avenue, London W5

Institute of Export
Export House, 14 Hallam Street, London W 1

The British Export Houses Association. The BEHA runs a
"marriage bureau" service to help exporters find an export house
appropriate to their needs. Advice and introductions can be
obtained from BEHA offices at the following addresses:
69 Cannon Street, London EC4
75 Harborne Road, Edgbaston, Birmingham 15
1 Old Hall Street, Liverpool 3
30 George Square, Glasgow C2
Ship Canal House, King Street, Manchester 2

Buying Office Association. *Export Buying Offices Association*
(EXBO), 54–62 Regent Street, London W1

Visiting Buyers. Details of overseas buyers arriving in the UK
are given in the weekly paper published by Overseas Trade News,
listing the name and firm of the buyer, his host in Britain and his
main purchase requirements.
Overseas Trade News, 30 Fleet Street, London EC4

Overseas Sales Organisation. The Overseas Marketing
Corporation was established by British finance houses with loan
capital provided by the British government, to market and sell
British products overseas, initially in western and eastern Europe.
Overseas Marketing Corporation Limited, 6 Arlington Street,
London SW1

STATE COMMISSION AGENCIES IN EASTERN EUROPE

Eastern Germany (German Democratic Republic)

Transinter Aussenhandelsvertretungen GmbH, 102 Berlin, Rosenthaler Strasse 40–41

Hungary

Agentura, Budapest 5, POB 187

Hungagent, Budapest 5, POB 542

Importtrade, Budapest 5, POB 542

Industria, Budapest 7, Akàcfa ut. 2b

Interag, Budapest 62, POB 184

Mercator, Budapest 5, Balassy Bàlint ut. 2

Universal, Budapest 1, Tàbor ut. 2–4

Zenit, Budapest 5, POB 17

Poland

Dynamo Ltd, Warsaw, Al. 1 Armii Wojska Polskiego 3, POB 332

Maciej Czarnecki & Co Ltd, Warsaw, Ul. Marszalkowska 87, POB 215

Mundial Ltd, Warsaw, Al. Armii Wojska Polskiego 3, POB 202

Polcomex Ltd, Warsaw, ul. Marszalkowska 140, POB 478

Poliglob Ltd, Warsaw, ul. Wspólna 3–5, POB 404

Timex Ltd, Warsaw, Al. 1 Armii Wojska Polskiego 3, POB 268

Transactor Ltd, Warsaw, Al. 1 Armii Wojska Polskiego 3

Transpol Ltd, Warsaw, Al. 1 Armii Wojska Polskiego 3, POB 280

Unitex SA, Warsaw, ul. Wspólna 3–5

Yugoslavia

Adria [*Representation of foreign firms*], Beograd, Trg Bratstva i Jedinstva 3

Astra [*Enterprise for international trade and representation*], Zagreb, Gajeva 5, POB 456

Agrooprema [*Export-import and representation of foreign firms*], Beograd, Balkanska 44, POB 694

Agroprogres [*Enterprise for representing of foreign firms*], Ljubljana, Kidriceva 1/IV POB 17

Agroservis [*Foreign representations*], Novi Sad, Vojvode Misica 2, POB 69

Auto-Hrvatska [*Export-import and representation of foreign firms*], Zagreb, Draskoviceva 47, POB 62–89

Autocommerce [*Representatives*], Ljubljana, Trdinova 4

Avtotehna [*Representatives of foreign firms*], Ljubljana, Celovska Cesta 38, POB 593–XI

Balkanija [*Representation of foreign firms*], Beograd, Gracanicka 14, POB 290

Brodomerkur [*Export-import and representation of foreign firms*], Split, Prvoboraca 35, POB 120

Brodokomerc [*Shipshandlers, export-import and representation of foreign firms*], Rijeka, Beogradski trg 3

Chemcolor [*Representation of foreign firms*], Zagreb, Proleterskih brigada 58a, POB 274

Commerce [*Representation of foreign firms*], Ljubljana, Titova 3/V, POB 48/1

Cosmos [*Foreign representations*], Ljubljana, Celovska cesta 32, POB 31–1

Delta [*Foreign representations*], Rijeka, Titov trg 32, POB 378

Dinara [*Foreign Agencies*], Beograd, Bircaninova 37, POB 810

Fabeg [*Representation of foreign firms*], Beograd, Trg Marksa i Engelsa 8, POB 524

Generalexport [*Enterprise for the promotion of foreign trade exchange*], Beograd, Djure Djakovica 31, POB 636

Hermes [*Representation of foreign firms*], Ljubljana, Titova cesta 25, POB 215-IV

Industrijaimport [*Export-import and representation of foreign firms*], Titograd, Proleterske brigade 36

Industrioservis [*Foreign representations and consignment stores*], Novi Sad, Bulevar Marsala Tita bb, POB 148

Interdalma [*Representation of foreign producers and consignment stores*], Split, Trg Republike 3, POB 221

Interexport[*Enterprise for international Trade*], Beograd, Kolarceva 8–10, POB 789

Interimpex [*Enterprise for the promotion of foreign trade exchange and representation of foreign firms*], Skopje, 11 Oktomvri 78/a, POB 204

Interkomerc [*General trade agency*], Beograd, Terazije 27/III, POB 15

Interpromet [*Representation of foreign firms and consignment stores*], Beograd, Prote Mateje 45, POB 328

Interservis [*Foreign representations*], Novi Sad, Dunavska 29, POB 34

Intertehna [*Representation of foreign firms*], Beograd, Kneza Milosa 47, POB 852

Intertrade [*Enterprise for international trade*], Ljubljana, Titova 1, POB 317–VI

Jugohemija [*Foreign representations*], Beograd, Kralja Milutina 10/a, POB 441

Jugoimport [*Enterprise for international trade*], Beograd, Knez Mihajlova 3, POB 308

Jugokomerc [*Foreign representations in Yugoslavia*], Sarajevo, JN Armije 19, POB 124

Jugomontana [*Representation of foreign firms*], Beograd, Obilićev venac 4, POB 85

Jugosanitarija [*Export-import and representation of foreign firms*], Zagreb, Djordjiceva 31, POB 22

Kip [*Export-import and representation of foreign trade exchange*], Ljubljana, Opekarska 13, POB 118

Konim [*Foreign industrial agency*], Ljubljana, Titova 38/VIII, POB 412

Kontaktor [*General representation of foreign producers*], Beograd, Knez Mihajlova 25, POB 811

Kontinental [*Foreign representations*], Beograd, Terazije 27/III, POB 167

Koteks [*Export-import and representation of foreign trade exchange*], Split, Prvoboraca 20, POB 245

Masinokomerc [*Foreign representations*], Beograd, Knez Mihailova 1–3, POB 232

Merkantile [*Representation of foreign trade exchange*], Zagreb, Svacicev trg 6

Merkur [*Representation of foreign firms*], Zagreb, Marticeva 14, POB 124

Omniauto [*Foreign representations*], Beograd, Borisa Kidriča 6/I, POB 33

Omnikomerc [*Foreign agency*], Beograd, Lole Ribara 22, POB 637

Progres [*Enterprise for the promotion of foreign trade exchange and representative*], Beograd, Knez Mihajlova 27, POB 527

Rapid [*Foreign representations*], Beograd, Knez Mihailova 7/I, POB 710

Tehnoservis [*Representation of foreign firms*], Beograd, Obilicev Venac 4

Tehno-Union [*Representation of foreign factories and consignment, stores*], Ljubljana, Vošnjakova 5, POB 01–347

Unikomerc [*Representation of foreign firms*], Zagreb, Varsavska 4, POB 02–5228

Univerzal [*Commercial representations*], Beograd, Majke Jevrosime 51, POB 30

Velebit [*Commercial and technical representation*], Zagreb, Draskovićeva 13, POB 458

Yugoslavia Commerce [*Representatives of foreign firms*], Beograd, Kneza Milosa 60, POB 385

Guide to Drawing up Contracts Between Parties Residing in Different Countries

By permission of the **International Chamber of Commerce**, 38 Cours Albert Ier, Paris 8e, France, the recommendations are reproduced here of the Commission on International Practice approved by the ICC Council in November 1960.

PRELIMINARY REMARKS

The present guide concerns the relationship between principals and commercial agents in the strict sense only, to the exclusion of any relations with third parties.

In commercial usage the term "agency" is often applied to relationships which may not be strictly agencies at all. An example which occurs is the use of the term "distributing agency" or some such equivalent term to describe the function of a distributor of manufactured goods which he obtains from a supplier under a sales agreement (usually an exclusive sales agreement). In such a relationship, the distributor does not come as an agent between a principal who sells and a customer who buys, but is himself buyer of the goods for resale to his own customers.

By the term "strict sense only" is meant a relationship where the agent, though bound to act within the scope of his authority, is not subject in the exercise of such authority to the direct control or supervision of the principal.

The niceties of legal interpretation, the incidence of customs and usages of the particular trade, the conflict of laws, and the economic problems are not within the province of the present Guide; but when negotiating a commercial agency contract the parties would do well to ascertain the exact position, as these matters are a fertile source of disputes in the field of international trade.

The laws of various countries of the world show considerable differences with regard to the legal status of commercial agents, and in many cases contain particularly detailed provisions governing the relationship between the principal and such an agent. Therefore, it is essential to procure that nothing contained in a commercial agency contract shall be repugnant to imperative provisions of the law of any country in which such a contract or any part thereof has to be carried into effect.

It should be borne in mind that an act of a commercial agent, done within the scope of his powers, may bind his principal. It may be found in certain countries that some such powers are either expressly or by implication vested in the agent by imperative provisions of the law, and that the contract may fall to be construed in accordance with that law and governed thereby.

In consequence, it is essential to consider, when drawing up the contract, whether the agent or any person acting under him has authority from the principal or by operation of law to assume any obligation or liability, or enter into any binding agreements, or give any guarantee, or make any warranty or representation whatsoever on behalf of the principal, or to settle any claim by or against the principal, or pledge the credit of the principal under the contract or, generally, to describe himself or hold himself out expressly or by implication as the agent or legal representative of the principal.

It is for the parties to the contract carefully to decide, in the light of the facts of each case, the various points which should be covered therein. The points to be covered and the way in which they should be covered will depend largely upon the extent to which the law of the country or countries concerned covers these matters and the extent to which the law leaves them freely to be expressed in the contract. But however short one may wish to make the contract by referring to the law on all matters not expressly settled by the contract, the application of general principles to the requirements of the particular case calls for a certain number of precise details.

It is appropriate to add a warning against the possible liability of the principal to tax in the contractual territory. In many countries a non-resident principal will be liable to tax if the agent has, and habitually exercises, a general authority to negotiate and conclude contracts on behalf of the principal. For instance, when a principal appoints an agent in a foreign country, with a fixed place of business therein and with power to make contracts on his behalf, the principal may be deemed to be carrying on business in that foreign country and be taxed accordingly. If the principal is a corporation, such corporation may be made subject to judicial process (even in matters quite unconnected with the agency) by service of a writ on the corporation at the address of its agency in such foreign country.

Experience has clearly shown, especially in the field of international trade, the expediency of reducing to writing the commercial agency contract and any amendments thereto; in certain countries the law requires that this be done. Moreover, both parties to the contract must realise the difficulty and the danger of drawing up such a contract without first seeking legal and fiscal advice, not only in the country of the principal, but also in each of the countries (if more than one) wherein the commercial agent is to have authority to act in that capacity for the principal.

1: HEADING OF THE CONTRACT

Legal Nature of the Agency Contract. In the title (or introductory part) of the contract, care should be taken clearly to state that it is a commercial agency contract, so as to avoid any doubt as regards the legal nature of the contract and the position of the parties thereunder.

2: PARTIES TO THE CONTRACT

A frequent source of confusion lies in uncertainty as to both the identity and the capacity of the parties to the contract. It is essential to ascertain not only the legal position or condition of each of the parties to the contract, e.g. an individual, a firm or partnership, a corporation, or as the case may be, but also that each person signing the document has capacity to contract.

The contract should clearly state the full names, addresses (the address being that to which all communications, including notices and judicial processes, should be sent), and capacities of each of the contracting parties and, in the case of firms, partnerships or corporations, the name or complete style of the firm, partnership, or corporation, its legal status, the date and place of its incorporation, head office, and so on.

A full description of the firm, partnership, or corporation is particularly important when the person executing the contract operates several undertakings with similar names and binds himself by his own signature in his business dealings.

Where more than one person is associated as agent, the agent being in partnership or otherwise associated, it should be the duty of the continuing agent to give notice to the principal of the retirement, prolonged illness, or death of his partner or associate.

It should be clearly stated whether the contract is to be assignable. In the affirmative, express provisions should be made to cover the circumstances in which the benefits and obligations of the contract may be assigned, e.g. to the principal's successor in business, or to an assignee of the agent previously approved by the principal, or as the case may be. Provision should be made for due notification of intention to assign.

If it is intended that the contract shall cancel and supersede all previous agreements between the principal and the agent relating to any matter or thing covered by the contract, except as regards the settlement of accounts and so on under such previous agreements, that should be clearly stated (see in this connection, Section 14).

3: AUTHENTIC TEXT

If the contract is written in two languages, the parties ought always to agree which of the two texts shall be the authentic text should difficulties of interpretation or construction arise.

4: DATES OF COMING INTO FORCE AND OF THE NORMAL EXPIRATION OF THE CONTRACT

As the parties reside in different countries, the contract may be signed on different dates; time limits may be stated in the contract.

Therefore, care should be taken to stipulate the date on which the contract shall come into force and, if it is to continue for a fixed period, then, the date on which it would normally expire. Further, and especially if the agency is granted for an unlimited time, it is advisable clearly to specify the events on the happening of which the contract shall cease and determine with or without any notice or other act by either of the parties (see, in this last connection, Section 12).

5: CONTRACTUAL PRODUCTS

It is important clearly to define the goods covered by the contract and, in some cases, the uses for which they are intended. If the principal sells more than one class of goods, the contract should state the class or classes included therein, to the exclusion of the others. If the principal subsequently extends his sales to other classes of goods, and it is intended that the contract shall confer upon the agent no rights of any kind with respect to such other classes, that should be clearly stated. It may be stipulated also that the agent shall be entitled to accept or to refuse the inclusion of such additional goods.

If the principal wishes to reserve the right to withdraw certain products from the contractual list during the continuance of the contract, that should be clearly stated.

If the parties desire, by means of periodic consultation or by other means, to fix maximum or minimum quantities to be supplied by the principal over stated periods, the necessary stipulation should be made under this heading. The matter of minimum sales is dealt with in Section 10, sub-section *o*.

6: CONTRACTUAL TERRITORY

The contract should clearly define the territory or territories (including or excluding any other country which may be associated with any such territory) in which the agent is entitled to act. It is important that the parties should give serious thought to this matter, as lack of precision may give rise to disputes between the agent and other agents of the principal as regards their respective territorial rights.

If the agent is not to be entitled to solicit and/or obtain orders from customers or prospective customers (being in the contractual territory) for goods which are intended or which the agent has reason to believe are intended for consumption or use outside the contractural territory, that should be clearly stated. This provision may be important, *inter alia*, for the protection of branded goods and trade marks in "third countries" and also for the protection of the principal from claims for commission from more than one agent in respect of the same sale.

7: SOLE AND EXCLUSIVE AGENCY RIGHTS

If the agent is to have the sole and exclusive right to represent the principal within the contractual territory, the parties should agree to what extent, if any, the principal may nevertheless reserve the right to operate in the territory, either himself or by means of his employees, with or without, as the case may be, the assistance of the agent.

The parties ought always to define the sole agent's rights in respect of orders placed direct with the principal. The principal may wish to reserve the right to supply certain named customers or certain categories of customers, or both (such as government departments, state-owned industries and so on) which approach him direct. It may happen that foreign buyers wish to place orders with the principal either during visits to the principal's country or through their purchasing offices in the principal's country, and it may then be inconvenient or commercially inexpedient to refer such orders back to the agent. Moreover, it will be found in some cases that states, government departments, and the like will deal with the principal only. If the agent is to receive commission on such transactions, that should be clearly stated.

8: CONTRACTUAL CLIENTELE

Whilst the agent may normally be authorised to choose, on his own initiative, the customers from whom he proposes to solicit orders in the contractual territory, it may sometimes be advisable to reach agreement upon the groups of customers to be or not to be canvassed (industry, wholesalers, retailers, official bodies, and so on).

In addition, it may be expedient in certain cases to append to the contract a list showing the customers of the principal in the contractual territory to whom the contractual goods or any of them had been sold before the coming into force of the contract, and the quantities and value of the goods so sold during the twelve months (or as the case may be) last preceding such time (see, in this connection, Section 9, sub-section *d* and Section 12)

9: RIGHTS AND OBLIGATIONS OF THE PRINCIPAL

(a) Acceptance of Orders.   The contract should state whether the agent may or may not make binding agreements on the principal's behalf in respect of orders obtained by the agent.

If all orders for goods shall be subject to acceptance by the principal, and he may refuse to accept any order without assigning any reason, it should be so stated in the contract. It is usual to provide that if the principal does not accept an order transmitted by the agent, the principal shall advise the agent accordingly, with all due dispatch.

The parties should provide for cases where there is silence or delay on the part of the principal in notifying acceptance or refusal of an order to the agent, and clearly state how far such silence or delay may be deemed, as between the principal and the agent, to be proof of acceptance or refusal.

(b) Information.   The activities of the agent in and about the promotion of sales usually conform to the production and sales programmes of the principal. Thus, the contract should stipulate the manner in which the agent shall be kept informed of the principal's sales policy and to what extent the principal shall send him the correspondence, documentation, and invoices exchanged between the principal and customers or potential customers within the contractual territory.

It is usual to provide that if the principal makes any changes in his price structure, terms of delivery, terms of payment, or standard conditions of sale, the agent shall be notified accordingly in due time. Care should also be taken to stipulate at what time

189

such changes shall become effective in the contractual territory.

(c) Establishment of a Factory within the Contractual Territory. If it is intended that during the continuance of the contract the principal shall be entitled, for economic, legal, or other reasons, to manufacture, cause to be manufactured, or grant licences to third parties to manufacture the contractual goods, or any of them, within the contractual territory, that eventuality should be considered and such provisions made in the contract as may be necessary or advisable for the purpose of defining the rights of the principal and the agent in such circumstances.

(d) Protection of Sole and Exclusive Rights. It is to the interest of both parties that the principal should use his best efforts to safeguard the sole and exclusive rights granted to the agent, especially to help him to resist any attempt on the part of third parties to interfere with these rights. Provisions appropriate to each particular case may be inserted in the contract (see Sections 7 and 10, sub-section *a*)

(e) Unfair Competition. The parties should consider whether it is of interest to stipulate that it is the duty of the principal to take appropriate steps to prevent unfair competition or the appearance on the market of infringements of his patents, trade marks, emblems, designs, models, or other similar industrial or commercial monopoly rights.

In any case, the contract may stipulate that the agent must advise the principal immediately of any infringements of these patents, trade marks, or other monopoly rights which may come to the agent's notice.

(f) Sales Aids, Advertising Matter. The contract should stipulate whether the principal is to provide the agent with samples, patterns, or other kinds of advertising material, and which party is to pay the cost of publicity and advertising material, excise duties, customs duties and clearance charges, if any, and the like, on such samples, patterns, and so on.

It should be considered whether samples or other advertising aids of permanent value should remain the property of the principal, and whether such a stipulation might be extended to restrict any lien on the goods granted to the agent by operation of law in respect of commission due, having in mind that in certain countries the agent has a right to retain such property until a sum owing to him by the principal is paid.

If the principal agrees to advertise the products and to participate with the agent in the expense of such advertising in the contractual territory, this should be clearly stated, and the terms of participation carefully defined.

If the principal agrees to furnish to the agent, with or without charge (as the case may be), such instruction books, folders, booklets, catalogues, blocks, cuts, and other sales promotion material, as the principal may deem necessary, this should be clearly stated.

(g) Travelling and Other Expenses. If the agent is to have a special allowance to cover travelling expenses, telephone calls, telegrams, or other expenses properly incurred in connection with the agency business, this should be clearly stated.

When it is desired that all the costs shall not be borne by one of the parties, it is necessary to stipulate that a stated fraction of clearly specified expenses shall be defrayed by one of the parties; the use of expressions like "participate in" or "in the main defray" such expenses, is a fertile source of dispute.

10: RIGHTS AND OBLIGATIONS OF THE AGENT

(a) Safeguarding of the Principal's Interests. Agency contracts frequently contain an express provision to the effect that the agent shall in and about the execution of his duties use every effort to safeguard the property, rights, and interests of his principal, in conformity with "best business practice," or some such term. Whilst it might perhaps go without saying that the agent must perform this duty, it may be advisable, in certain circumstances, to insert a clause to this effect.

Suitable provision may also be made under this heading for the crediting of any money received by the agent on behalf of the principal to a separate banking account. This provision may be desirable in order to protect the principal's money from aggregation with the assets of his agent in the event of bankruptcy, sequestration, and so on.

(b) The Power to Enter into Binding Agreements. The contract should expressly state whether the agent has the power to enter into binding agreements on behalf of the principal and, in the affirmative, to what extent (see also Section 9, sub-section *a*).

(c) Capacity to Act in the Name of the Principal. It may be advisable, in the interests of all concerned, to stipulate that it is the agent's duty, when dealing with third parties, to act in such manner as to avoid any ambiguity and dispute as to the source, nature and extent of his authority.

(d) Observance of Conditions of Sale. The parties should ascertain to what extent the law of the contractual territory allows the agent to be bound to comply with any instructions of the principal concerning prices, terms of delivery, terms of payment, conditions of sale, and so on, and make such provision in the contract as may be necessary to avoid any confusion in this respect.

(e) Forbidding Competition. If it is deemed necessary expressly to prohibit the agent from dealing in goods of a type competing or likely to compete with the contractual products, the stipulation to this effect may extend to cover either the life of the contract, or the period following the expiration or the earlier termination of the contract, or both of these periods.

With regard to the period following the termination of the contract, whether by effluxion of time, by act of either party, or otherwise, it is important that any restriction should be limited in time and space and that the exact nature of the prohibited acitivities should be stipulated.

The parties should consider whether the agent shall be entitled to accept new agencies likely to compete with those granted by the contract. In the negative, it would be useful to append to the contract a list of the agencies (if any) already held by the agent at the time of the signing of the contract.

The prohibition should not serve to injure or unduly to limit the agent's professional activities, and the parties should remember that the statute law and the practice of courts in certain countries are often at pains to maintain the limited character of the prohibition.

The parties should consider to what extent the agent may be

entitled to compensation if the prohibition continues to operate after the expiration or the earlier termination of the contract.

(f) Purchases for Own Account. The contract may stipulate to what extent, if any, the agent shall be entitled to buy from the principal for his own account. In the affirmative, it would be advisable to specify the conditions under which the agent may buy and resell for his own account and at what price (see in this connection the Preliminary Remarks, on page 183).

(g) Consignment Stocks. The term "consignment" implies that the stocks belong to the consignor (the principal); he may thus require, if he so desires, that the goods be returned, just as the consignee (the agent) is entitled to return the goods unsold.

The parties ought always expressly to agree on the terms to govern all matters relating to consignment stocks.

Consignments stocks should be insured. The contract should stipulate the manner in which the "insurance" clause is to be applied and which party is to pay the premium.

Similarly, the contract should stipulate who is liable for all other expenses incurred in connection with the storage and maintenance of the stock.

The conditions for the sale of consignment stocks, the incidence of price fluctuations and to whom the purchase price is payable, should be clearly stated. If payment is to be made to the agent, it should be stipulated how he is to settle with the principal.

Special provisions are needed to cover the case of consignment stocks sold on credit terms.

It may be stipulated that at certain intervals the agent is to submit a list of the stock on hand, certified as true and accurate by him. It is in the interests of both parties to insert in their contract clauses governing the replenishing and handling of the consignment stocks. It should be stipulated that the principal has the right to check the stock or to cause the stock to be checked, at any time.

It must be borne in mind that in some countries the fact of having created a consignment stock lays the principal open to being regarded as carrying on business in the country, and to being taxed accordingly (see in this connection the Preliminary Remarks, page 183).

The contract may also contain clauses concerning the duty of the agent to take all necessary steps to safeguard the principal's right of ownership of goods consigned.

In cases where the consigned stock is stored on premises belonging to a third party, such party may have a lien on the goods for unpaid rent and the like; this matter should receive consideration.

On the other hand, neither the principal nor the agent should be entitled to pledge or otherwise charge the consignment stock as security.

If the law of the contractual territory makes the legal effect of the consignment contract dependent on the actual setting apart of the consigned goods, the agent's duty in this connection should be clearly stated.

(h) Service after Sale and Spare Parts.   If the agent is expected to keep spare parts in stock or to give his customers special after-sales service, or both, the scope of these obligations should be stated, if possible, in the contract, and also the amount of any remuneration, over and above his commission, that may be payable by the principal to the agent in return for such services.

(i) Commercial and Financial Information.   If it is to be the agent's duty to keep the principal currently informed, to the best of the agent's knowledge and belief, of all such commercial conditions and changes in the market and in the financial status of the customers or prospective customers, as may be of importance for the business of the principal, that should be clearly stated.

(j) Arrangement of Sales Work.   As the agent exercises an independent activity, he is at liberty reasonably to decide the manner in which his sales organisation shall function. This freedom of the agent is thus laid down as a rule. In this connection, it may be stipulated that the agent shall be alone responsible for his sub-agents, whose total remuneration shall be paid by him. The rule being so, it is normal that the principal should assume no liability towards sub-agents, who will be in contact with the agent only, it being understood that as the principal will accept no obligation towards the sub-agents, he may not interfere with their work.

If there is to be any restriction placed on the liberty of the agent to appoint sub-agents, that should be clearly stated.

(k) Insolvent Customers. An express stipulation prohibiting agents from obtaining orders from customers known to be insolvent may be useless since this prohibition seems to flow from the agent's general obligation to safeguard the principal's interests, as well as from his duty to report, as provided in sub-sections *a* and *i* of this present Section.

However, the contract may stipulate that, as far as possible, the agent shall satisfy himself by means of proper inquiries, as to the solvency of customers whose orders he transmits to the principal.

(l) The Principal's Industrial Property Rights. It may be made clear in the contract that it follows from the general obligations incumbent on the agent that it is part of his duty promptly to inform the principal of any infringement that may come to his notice in the course of his work, in respect of patent rights, designs and models, trade marks, emblems, and the like, being the property of or used by the principal, and to assist the principal, at the principal's request, in taking the necessary steps to defend these rights.

Unless otherwise stipulated in the contract, this assistance should not involve any obligation on either party to institute legal proceedings against the infringer.

Subject to the same reservation, it is not the agent's duty to have the principal's trade marks, patents, and other monopoly rights registered on the latter's behalf; if, however, such a clause is necessary, it is important that the contract should stipulate in whose name the registration is to be made.

The agent may be entitled to the repayment of any expenses incurred by him in these connections.

Where the agent is to be permitted to use any trade mark which is the property of the principal, or used by him, care should be taken to prevent a prescriptive right from arising. The contract may stipulate that nothing therein contained shall be construed to authorise the agent: (i) to use that trade mark as the style or name, or as part of the style or name, of any firm, partnership, or corporation; (ii) to apply the same to any goods other than the contractual products; and (iii) at any time after the termination of contract whether by effluxion of time, by act of either party, or otherwise, to apply that trade mark to any goods or to any other use whatsoever.

(m) Collection of Sums Due. In cases where customers do not pay directly to the principal and where the agent is responsible for collecting the sums due, his powers and the amount of the remuneration, if any, to which he shall be entitled in this connection, should be clearly stated, due regard being had to the warning sounded in the Preliminary Remarks.

(n) *Del Credere*. If the agent undertakes to work on *del credere* basis, either because this is customary in the particular trade or for any other special reason, the contract should clearly state the conditions, such as the amount of the guarantee, the exact nature and extent of the agent's liability under such guarantee, the prior attempts to be made to collect the sums due, the nature of the transactions giving rise to the guarantee, the date at which the debt shall be deemed to be bad, and so on.

In the interests of both parties, it should be clearly stated: (i) to what extent, if any, the principal may modify the terms of payment without the consent of the agent, and (ii) that the principal shall notify the agent of any default, without delay.

It may be stipulated that the liability (if any) of the agent shall be limited to cases where the agent has obtained the order for the goods and such order has been accepted by the principal, to the exclusion of the indirect sales (or any of them) contemplated in Section 7 above. The agent may be granted the power of direct collection and of taking protective measures in an emergency.

The contract may stipulate a special *del credere* remuneration and fix the date or dates at which this special remuneration shall accrue and become payable to the agent.

(o) Minimum Sales. The contract may provide that the agent shall guarantee a certain minimum sales turn-over in respect of goods sold over a given period. There may be doubts as to the value and expediency of such guarantees, but the matter calls for consideration.

It is important to stipulate the consequences to the agent for his failure to achieve the minimum sales, and to consider the incidence of certain events, such as non-acceptance of an order by the principal, his failure to deliver the goods, imposition of import restrictions, and so on.

A higher rate of commission or a supplementary commission

may be stipulated when a minimum sale is guaranteed, or when the minimum is exceeded.

(p) Guaranteed Minimum Income. The principal may agree to guarantee the agent a certain income, for example in cases where the latter has relinquished other agencies for the purpose of devoting himself solely or mainly to the contractual agency, or for other reasons.

11: COMMISSION

The basis of calculation of the commission and the rate of same should be clearly stipulated.

The commission may be calculated on the net amount or the gross amount of the invoice to the customer, or otherwise, as the case may be. If the net amount is used as a basis, the contract should specify the various items of costs such as freight, insurance, discount, taxes, packing, and the like, to be deducted.

If it is a sole agency agreement, the contract may stipulate that the agent is entitled to commission on all orders received indirectly as well as direct from the contractual territory (see Section 7). If it is not a sole agency agreement, the contract should stipulate to what extent the agent shall be entitled to commission when he has taken no part, or acted only partially, in the conclusion of the business, or when he has taken part in the initial stages, but subsequently the transactions have been settled directly between the customer and the principal without his further intervention.

Moreover, it is desirable to stipulate whether the agent is entitled to a commission on transactions concluded through him but executed outside the contractual territory, so as to avoid disputes between agents assigned to several areas when the same transaction encroaches on these areas.

The contract shall stipulate when the right to a commission shall accrue: when the order is transmitted or accepted, when the goods are delivered, at the time the purchase price is paid, or as the case may be. Likewise, the contract should stipulate when the commission shall become payable.

It should also be stipulated how far the amount of the commission shall be affected by subsequent events: cancellation of an order, reduction in the price, failure of the principal to deliver the goods, the bankruptcy or insolvency of the buyer, and so on. The intention of the parties in this regard should be clearly stated.

The contract should stipulate whether the agent is to be paid commission only on orders which he actually obtains himself or also on repeat orders in the obtaining of which he plays no positive part. In either case, a definite period should be fixed for termination of the right to commission, because if such definite period is not stated there is a danger that commission might be payable on all repeat orders.

It would also be advisable to stipulate the currency in which the commission is to be calculated and paid and, if necessary, the rate of exchange applicable.

The contract should stipulate when payments of commissions shall be made (usually it will be quarterly or half-yearly, more rarely monthly or yearly). The principal should supply the agent with a list of orders received from the contractual territory, and in respect of which the agent is entitled to a commission. The agent could exercise a check or cause a check to be made on the list by an inspection of the relevant books and vouchers.

12: EXPIRATION OR EARLIER TERMINATION— COMPENSATION FOR LOSS OF CLIENTELE

The contract may be made for a definite or an indefinite period. If an indefinite period is chosen, it should be stipulated that the contract can be terminated subject to such previous notice (sent by registered letter post) as the parties may agree.

If it is intended that there shall be a trial period during which the contract may be terminated without notice, that should be clearly stated.

It may be stipulated that certain events, such as bankruptcy, voluntary liquidation, or winding up by order of the court, reorganisation, merger, assignment of portfolio of customers, shall either entail automatic termination or give either party the right to terminate.

When either of the parties is an individual or both parties are individuals, and the contract is not assignable (see Section 2, fifth paragraph), it should be stipulated whether the transfer of the business or the death of either party shall entail the automatic termination of the contract or whether, on the contrary, such transfer merely gives the other party the right to terminate the contract.

Certain effects may survive termination, according to the provisions of the contract. Thus, for example, orders received but not executed during the continuance of the contract may call for the payment of a commission (see, in this connection, Section 10, sub-section *e*).

The parties ought always to agree on matters relating to the preservation of trade secrets or to abstention from acts of competition (such as those listed under Section 10, sub-section *e*) after the expiration or earlier termination of the contract.

It may be stipulated that each of the parties may terminate the contract "for justifiable reasons," such as may be specified in the contract.

In the event of termination of the contract by the principal for a reason other than a wrongful act on the part of the agent, the contract may stipulate that the agent shall be entitled to compensation (e.g. for the loss of clientele), and provision may be made, where suitable, for the basis on which such compensation shall be assessed. In certain countries the agent may be legally entitled to receive compensation either for loss of clientele or for some other good and sufficient reason on the termination of the contract by effluxion of time, by act of either party or otherwise.

To help assessment of compensation it may be convenient to append to the contract a statement, certified by the two parties as being true and accurate, showing in particular as regards the contractual territory:

(i)   A list of customers in the contractual territory at the date of the coming into force of the contract; and

(ii) The quantities of goods (tonnage, volume and number) sold during the twelve months last preceding that date

—as mentioned in the last paragraph of Section 8 above.

13: CONFLICT OF LAWS AND OF COMPETENT JURISDICTION

The parties ought always to agree on the law to govern the contract and the law so chosen should be stipulated in the contract.

Under the law of some countries, the agency contract is governed by the law of the country where the agent carries on his business.

The same reservation applies to the clause regarding competent jurisdiction. Normally, the parties may stipulate that disputes arising out of the contract shall be submitted either to ordinary courts of law or to arbitration. Thus, generally speaking, it may be in the interests of the parties to insert in the contract the arbitration clause of the International Chamber of Commerce or of any other body providing similar guarantees. However, under the law of certain countries, special courts exist with exclusive rights to deal with such cases.

14: GENERAL CLAUSE

The parties ought always to insert a suitably worded clause at the end of their contract to the effect that there are no other agreements in existence between the parties and that the whole of the terms between the parties are set out in the contract.

THE ICC ARBITRATION CLAUSE

One of the ICC's main activities is to provide, through its arbitration clause, international facilities for avoiding or resolving business disputes.

The ICC arbitration clause states that "All disputes arising in connection with the present contract shall be finally settled under the Rules of Conciliation and Arbitration of the International Chamber of Commerce by one or more arbitrators appointed in accordance with the Rules."

Copies of these Rules, and also of the Guide to ICC Arbitration, are available from ICC Headquarters, 38 Cours Albert Ier, Paris 8e, or from any of its forty-one National Committees throughout the world.

Adding the ICC arbitration clause to foreign contracts can guarantee a rapid and effective method of settling a business dispute, and can also have a deterrent effect, tending to prevent such disputes from arising.

The parties can agree to submit a dispute to ICC arbitration even if the contract does not contain the ICC arbitration clause.

APPENDIX 7

Specimen Agency Agreements

These specimen contracts are only to act as a guide to the way they can be drawn up. There is great danger in simply following an existing specimen without giving full thought to the essential clauses which should be included to meet the special requirements of each relationship. (See Appendix 6 and Chapters 7 and 8.)

By kind permission of the **Institute of Export**, Export House, 14 Hallam Street, London W1, the Institute's summary of essential clauses and three specimen agreements are reproduced below.

TYPES OF AGENCY AGREEMENTS

Three main types of agreement may be needed by an exporter engaged in trade with a number of overseas territories. They are: (*a*) The agent may act as principal in the territory; that is to say, he will buy for his own account and be responsible for payment of all the goods he orders. He must of course carry a reasonable stock of his principal's goods. This form of agency is from the manufacturer's point of view a simple and safe one on several grounds, but it may entail the necessity for special, low export prices being quoted.

(*b*) The arrangement may be one by which the agent buys for stock, for his own account, the most popular and current lines made by the manufacturer, while the latter agrees to lay down in the country stocks on consignment of certain lines which may not at first show promise of speedy movement. In the case of such consignment stocks it is is most essential that in the agency agreement it be clearly established within the law governing the interpretation of its terms and also that of the country for which the agency is granted, should there be any difference, that the goods remain the absolute property of the principal until sold by the agent and that any sum collected in payment for such consignment stock is held in trust for the principal except those moneys on account of commission, or other direct outlays by the agent which it is agreed are due to him. This point requires careful consideration and involves the principal in payment by him of shipping charges, freight, insurance, export and import agent's stores, and storage and insurance charges while the goods remain in stock unsold. In some countries payment by the agent of any one of these items entitles him to property in the goods to the extent that, in the event of his bankruptcy, they may be seized, or disposed of, by his creditors, the principal ranking only as an unsecured creditor.

(c) The agent may act solely on a commission basis either for the disposal of the consignment stocks referred to above, or for the collection of order on an indent basis. Here the agent may carry the whole, part, or none, of the *del credere* risk. His remuneration will, of course, be fixed at a rate commensurate wilth the financial risk he assumes. It is desirable that the agent shall always have some stake financially, otherwise there is the temptation to sell indiscriminately to all and sundry without discretion for the principal's interest.

ESSENTIAL CLAUSES IN AN AGENCY AGREEMENT

The following are the subjects which, if eventual friction between the parties is to be averted, should be considered by the exporter and, if appropriate, find a place in a properly drawn-up agreement between a manufacturer and an agent abroad:

1 Statement of Parties to the Agreement

2 Purpose of the Agreement.
One party agrees to appoint the other as agent and the other agrees to act as agent, subject to the terms and conditions stated.

3 Description of the Goods the Subject of the Agency. Here the general statement is usually sufficient—possibly by reference to the manufacturer's lists—so long as it defines clearly the limits covered. Principal may reserve the right to discontinue manufacture of any of the goods upon giving reasonable notice to the agent.

4 The Territory to be Covered. Depending upon its extent, this may be confined to the precincts of a single town; be wholly included within, or entirely cover, the boundaries of a single country, or state; be defined by latitude and longitude; be coincident with the limits of a mandated territory, etc.

5 The Duties of the Principal. Such duties as are not referred to in other clauses of the agreement should be clearly stated. Principal's right to deal with other agents, or to make sales to the territory other than through the agent, to be defined. Principal to refer all inquiries received direct by him, to the agent.

6 The Duties of the Agent. To be clearly laid down without ambiguity, where not referred to elsewhere in the agreement. Is agent permitted to handle, sell, or have any interest in, goods of a competitive nature? Agent shall not knowingly sell goods the subject of the agreement for export from the territory. Possibility of the agent making sales of goods of a competitive nature directly to assist sale of principal's lines.

Agents shall, or may, by nameplate at their office or on their letter-heading, inform public that they are agents or sole agents of principal. Agent shall sell goods under principal's descriptions only; shall not apply to them any warranty other than that permitted by principal. Agent shall at all reasonable times afford accredited representative of principal access to the offices and warehouses of the agent and facilitate inspection of his books.

7 Exceptions, Reserves, or Restrictions. Certain customers in the territory, or selling to it, such as London buying houses, old-standing accounts, etc. Other exclusions may arise from convention arrangements, trade agreements, quota participation, and the like.

8 Method of Quoting by the Principal. Whether f.o.b.

c. and f., c.i.f., c.i.f. landed, c.i.f. and c., c.i.f. delivered agent's go-down duty paid, or otherwise.

9 Method of Purchase and Sale by the Agent. Agent may buy for his own account from the principal and resell as a dealer, or merchant. Agent may place orders with the principal, leaving the latter to invoice clients direct. Does agent bear *del credere* risk for sales outright, or from consignment stocks?

Prices for sales from consignment stocks by the agent should be the best obtainable at time of sale and should not be less than those authorised from time to time by the principal. The agent to supply full specification of goods required with all orders and to give complete shipping instructions as to port and time of delivery, marks, etc. If necessary, sale prices to be based on c.i.f. prices quoted by the principal and in no case to be less than those authorised by the principal, who thus retains in his own hands control of sale prices in the market.

10 Goods on Consignment. It may be desirable to maintain consignment stocks in the territory. The advantage of stock delivery as against shipment is obvious and may not only increase sales but bring about higher realisations.

How consignment goods are to be delivered by the principal. Agents to pay landing charges, duty, cartage, warehousing, insurance, etc, and recover by debiting the principal in current account. Goods on consignment to remain the property of the principal while unsold. How goods are to be disposed of upon termination of the agreement. Agent not to sell from consignment stocks other than as agent of the principal.

11 Stocks and Spares Maintained in the Territory. Whether on consignment, or purchased outright by the agent. Disposal of these on termination of the agency.

12 Cost of Cables. Whether to be borne by the principal wholly, or each party to bear the cost of his own.

13 Force Majeure. Principals free from responsibility for late delivery if due to *force majeure*. Principal shall advise the agent promptly and, where necessary, supply certificate.

14   Optional, or Permissive Clause.   If the principal cannot meet competition in any particular case, or for any reason should be unable temporarily to supply goods, may the agent purchase elsewhere?

15   Commission.   To be stated for different forms of orders placed and sales made by the agent and orders received by the principal either direct from the territory or through London. It must be made clear on what figure the commission is to be paid, e.g. "on the f.o.b. price, excluding packing."

16   Books of Account.   The agent to keep regular books of account and in respect of consignment sales render periodical account sales, the period to be stated. For orders placed by the agent for his own account he shall remit against receipt of documents. The agent to credit the principal in current account with consignment sales and remit monthly, quarterly, or as exchange becomes available, where exchange restrictions exist.

17   Overprice.   Where the agent sells at prices in excess of those minima normally based on c.i.f. quotations made and authorised by the principal, allocation of such overprices between the parties. Sales of this nature to be limited to figures which will not adversely affect sales of the principal's goods.

18   Charges for Propaganda and How Borne.   Expenses and nature of advertising, special propaganda, etc, if for account of the principal in whole, or part, to be subject to the principal's authorisation.

19   Periodical Reports.   The agent to submit regular periodical reports on his activities and territory and the principal to keep the agent constantly informed of changes and developments in his manufactures.

20   General Conditions.   The agent shall not pledge the principal's credit without consent, nor commence legal proceedings in the name of the principal. The agent shall not divulge to others information relating to principal's business.

Any other conditions not mentioned elsewhere in agreement.

21 Duration. To be stated; whether firm for any period without right to determine, or, if the latter, term of notice to exercise right and whether this be for both principal and agent.

22 Breach of Agreement. If either party be guilty of, or countenance, breach of agreement, the party not in default has right to determine either summarily, or under clause 21.

Similarly, where either the agent or principal, goes into liquidation, other than voluntarily for the purpose of reconstruction, or makes a composition with his creditors, the action to be taken.

23 Law Governing the Agreement and Arbitration. This should be stated and also the method to be employed in referring to arbitration any dispute which cannot be amicably settled.

24 Assignment. The benefits and obligations of the agreement may not be assigned other than by common consent of the parties to it.

Practically all the considerations which may be expected usually to arise in drawing up a normal type of agency agreement have been indicated in the preceding twenty-four clauses. It does not follow, of course, that these in their entirety are necessary, or even applicable, to every agreement, while conversely it may be found essential upon occasion to augment their number to meet some special circumstance.

As an illustration of the construction of typical agency agreements, there follow three examples which, because of their normality and actual use, may be proffered as standard agency agreements. These are suitable for (1) a merchant house, having its own organisation in the territory overseas, acting as agents; (2) an agent working on consignment account; and (3) an exclusive sole agent, resident overseas. [Prepared by the Institute of Export.]

SPECIMEN AGREEMENT 1

Suitable for exclusive and sole agents representing manufacturers overseas

AN AGREEMENT made this   day of
19   BETWEEN
whose Registered office is situate at
(hereinafter
called "the Principal") of the one part and
(hereinafter
called "the Agent") of the other part.
WHEREBY IT IS AGREED as follows:
1   The Principal appoints the Agent as and from the
to be its sole Agent in
(hereinafter called
"the area") for the sale of
manufactured by the Principal and such other goods and merchandise (all of which are hereinafter referred to as "the goods") as may hereafter be mutually agreed between them.
2   The Agent will during the term of   years (and thereafter until determined by either party giving three months' previous notice in writing) diligently and faithfully serve the Principal as its Agent and will endeavour to extend the sale of the goods of the Principal within the area and will not do anything that may prevent such sale or interfere with the development of the Principal's trade in the area.
3   The Principal will from time to time furnish the Agent with a statement of the minimum prices at which the goods are respectively to be sold and the Agent shall not sell below such minimum price but shall endeavour in each case to obtain the best price obtainable.
4   The Agent shall not sell any of the goods to any person, company, or firm residing outside the area, nor shall he knowingly sell any of the goods to any person, company, or firm residing within the area with a view to their exportation to any other country or area without the consent in writing of the Principal.
5   The Agent shall not during the continuance of the Agency hereby constituted sell goods of a similar class or such as would or might compete or interfere with the sale of the Principal's

goods either on his own account or on behalf of any other person, company, or firm whomsoever.

6 Upon receipt by the Agent of any order for the goods the Agent will immediately transmit such order to the Principal who (if such order is accepted by the Principal) will execute the same by supplying the goods direct to the customer.

7 Upon the execution of any such order the Principal shall forward to the Agent a duplicate copy of the invoice sent with the goods to the customer and in like manner shall from time to time inform the Agent when payment is made by the customer to the Principal.

8 The Agent shall duly keep an account of all orders obtained by him and shall every three months send in a copy of such account to the Principal.

9 The Principal shall allow the Agent the following commissions (based on f.o.b. United Kingdom values) in respect of all orders obtained direct by the Agent in the area which have been accepted and executed by the Principal. The said commission shall be payable every three months on the amounts actually received by the Principal from the customers.

10 The Agent shall be entitled to commission on the terms and conditions mentioned in the last preceding clause on all export orders for the goods received by the Principal through Export Merchants Indent Houses, Branch Buying offices of customers, and Head Offices of customers situate in the United Kingdom of Great Britain, Northern Ireland and the Irish Free State for export into the area. Export orders in this clause mentioned shall not include orders for the goods received by the Principals from and sold delivered to customers' principal place of business outside the area although such goods may subsequently be exported by such customers into the area, excepting where there is conclusive evidence that such orders which may actually be transmitted via the Head Office in England are resultant from work done by the Agent with the customers.

11 Should any dispute arise as to the amount of commission payable by the Principal to the Agent the same shall be settled by the Auditors for the time being of the Principal whose certificate shall be final and binding on both the Principal and the Agent.

12 The Agent shall not in any way pledge the credit of the Principal.

13 The Agent shall not give any warranty in respect of

the goods without the authority in writing of the Principal.

14   The Agent shall not without the authority of the Principal collect any moneys from customers.

15   The Agent shall not give credit to or deal with any person, company, or firm which the Principal shall from time to time direct him not to give credit to or deal with.

16   The Principal shall have the right to refuse to execute or accept any order obtained by the Agent or any part thereof and the Agent shall not be entitled to any commission in respect of any such refused order or part thereof so refused.

17   All questions of difference whatsoever which may at any time hereafter arise between the parties hereto or their respective representatives touching these presents or the subject matter thereof or arising out of or in relation thereto respectively and whether as to construction or otherwise shall be referred to arbitration in England in accordance with the provision of the Arbitration Act 1950 or any re-enactment or statutory modification thereof for the time being in force.

18   This Agreement shall in all respects be interpreted in accordance with the Laws of England.

AS WITNESS the hands of the parties hereto the day and year first hereinbefore written.

(Signatures)

SPECIMEN AGREEMENT 2

Suitable for merchant firm having its own Branches or Head Office in overseas territory, buying as Principals and paying cash for stock, at time of shipment

AN AGREEMENT made this   day of
19   BETWEEN
whose Registered office is situate at

(hereinafter
called "the Principal") of the one part and

(hereinafter
called "the Agent") of the other part.
WHEREBY IT IS AGREED AS FOLLOWS:

1 The Company appoints the Agents to be its Sole Representatives throughout the

(hereinafter referred to as "the Agency Territory") for the sale of the Company's   and the Agents hereby accept such appointment.

2 The Agency shall be deemed to have commenced on the day of   and shall continue in force until determined as hereinafter provided.

3 The Company will invoice all goods supplied to the Agents at Company's lowest prices applicable from time to time in the Agency Territory less the usual trade discount, and cash discount if any, or at the special prices quoted for particular requirements. All goods supplied pursuant to this agreement shall be paid for in London by the Agents as and when shipped.

4 The Company will refer to the Agents all inquiries and/or orders which they may receive for their

for shipment to the Agency Territory, for instructions as to how to deal with such direct business.

Upon all orders received by the Company direct from the Agency Territory or through other British or Continental merchants or other buying authorities for shipment to that Territory, the execution of which has been sanctioned by the Agents, the Company will allow the Agents a commission of   per cent on net cash received in respect of same.

5 The Agents shall not handle or be interested in any competitive products without the consent—to be previously obtained—of the Principals.

Where, however, the Agents act as Buying Agents for a Company or individuals they are to be allowed, without reference to the Principals, to carry out the instructions of any of their Principals who definitely request them to buy competitor's goods.

6 All commissions which shall be due to the Agents shall be credited quarterly on the 31 March, 30 June, 30 September, and the 31 December in each year. Quarterly commission statements shall be rendered by the Company to the Agents as soon as possible after each Quarter Day.

7 The Company shall keep the Agents supplied free of charge with their standard catalogues and literature, and also furnish estimates when necessary for the said Agents to pass on to intending customers.

8   The Company or the Agents may at any time terminate the Agency by giving to the other or sending by registered post to the last known place of business of the other six months' notice in writing of their desire so to do and such six months shall begin to run from date when the notice shall be received.

9   In the case of any difference or dispute arising between the Company and the said Agents it shall be referred to arbitration in England in accordance with the provisions contained in the Arbitration Act 1950 or any statutory modification thereof.

IN WITNESS WHEREOF we the parties signed this Agreement in duplicate this   day of
In the presence of

....By ....

In the presence of

.... By ....

SPECIMEN AGREEMENT 3

Suitable for agents appointed overseas to whom stocks are shipped on consignment account

AN AGREEMENT made this   day of
19   BETWEEN
whose Registered office is situate at
                                                                (hereinafter
called "the Principal") of the one part and
                                                                (hereinafter called
"the Agent") of the other part.

WHEREBY IT IS AGREED AS FOLLOWS:

1   The Principals hereby appoint the Agent as their *del credere* sole agent for the sale in (the territory)   of
                                      (the goods) and the Agent accepts the appointment on the terms hereinafter defined.

2   This Agreement shall come into operation as from
                                      and shall continue in force for one year certain and thereafter until terminated by either party giving to the other   calendar months' notice in writing

expiring on any date provided always that either party may determine it summarily if the other party fails to carry out the terms of the Agreement, or goes into liquidation other than voluntarily for the purpose of reconstruction, or is wound up, or makes a composition with his creditors.

3   The Agent shall at all times use his best endeavours to develop the sale of the Principal's goods the subject of the agency within the territory and undertakes not to sell, or offer for sale, any goods competing with those of the Principals.

4   The Principals shall be free to sell the aforesaid
                    without the territory of the Agent and shall not be obliged to pay commission to the Agent on
shipped into the said territory unless sold by the Agent.

5   The Principals shall ship on consignment reasonable quantities of the goods to the Agent against indents. All such goods on consignment together with the necessary containers shall remain the absolute property of the Principals until delivered to the Buyer under safe contract. The Agent shall pay landing charges, duty, cartage, warehousing costs and insurance on account of the Principals and shall recover these by debiting the Principals in current account.

6   The Agent undertakes that no charge, or lien, shall be created on the goods so consigned.

7   As consideration for the Agent's service hereunder the Principals shall pay the Agent commission at the rate of
per centum which shall be calculated on the c.i.f. invoice value of all   sold in the said territory by the Agent. The Agent undertakes to indemnify the Principals against all default by purchasers in payment for the Principals' goods after sale and delivery.

8   The Agent undertakes not to pass on to the buyer any part of his commission, but may divide it with his appointed distributors where he can control their selling prices.

9   The Agent shall keep and maintain proper books of account and shall remit quarterly to the Principals statements and the sterling equivalent of the net proceeds of sales of the goods which have been made by him subject to retention by him of the commission provided for in Clause 7 hereof and those charges payable by him under Clauses 5, 10, and 11 and properly to be debited to the Principals.

212

10   Each of the parties hereto shall bear his own expenses other than those specifically payable by the other except that charges incurred by the Agent for cables and telegrams properly dispatched in the conduct of the business shall be refunded to him by the Principals.

11   Sales literature shall be supplied free to the Agent by the Principals and a reasonable allowance for advertisement and propaganda to be mutually agreed upon shall be paid for by the Principals.

12   The Agent shall be free by nameplate at his office, or on his letter-heading, or in other manner approved by the Principals, to inform the public that he is the sole agent of the Principals during the continuance of this agreement.

13   Determination of this agreement shall relieve the Principals of any right of claim against them by the Agent for any commission upon sales made by the Principals to customers introduced to them by the Agent during the existence of the agreement, or in respect of deliveries made against contracts effected before the determination of the agreement.

14   This agreement shall be interpreted according to the Laws of England and any dispute between the parties shall be settled by arbitration as provided for by the rules laid down by the Arbitration Act, 1950, or any statutory modification thereof.

AS WITNESS the hands of the Parties, etc.

With grateful acknowledgement to the **London Chamber of Commerce**, 69 Cannon Street, London EC4, another specimen agreement for an agent in an overseas market is reproduced here.

MEMORANDUM OF AGREEMENT made this   day of
One thousand nine hundred and
BETWEEN   of   (hereinafter
referred to as "The Principals") of the one part, and
          of   (hereinafter referred
to as "The Agents") of the other part.
WHEREBY IT IS AGREED AS FOLLOWS:

1   The Principals hereby appoint the Agents as their sole Agents
in   (hereinafter called "the territory")
for the sale of   for a period of
years from the date hereof and thereafter until determined by either
party giving   months notice in writing
2   The Principals agree to pay Commission at the rate of
per cent upon the net f.o.b. (or c.i.f., etc) value of all goods
delivered to the territory and paid for by the buyers, whether the
orders for such goods shall have been received from the Agents
or by the Principals direct, or in any manner whatsoever, and after
the termination of the agency the Agents shall be entitled to commission at the above mentioned rate on orders obtained by them
and accepted by the Principals during the period of this Agreement
although payment for the goods had not been made by the buyer
before the date of termination.
3   The Agents shall not sell the goods or any part thereof to any
buyer outside the territory nor shall they knowingly sell the goods
or any part thereof to any buyer residing within the territory with
a view to their exportation to any other country or territory without the consent in writing of the Principals, and the Agents shall
not during the continuance of the Agency sell other goods of the
same class or so similar to compete with the sale of the Principal's
products.
4   Commission statements shall be made up to the last day of each
quarter, and shall include the commission on all invoices paid up
to and including the last day of the quarter. Commission statements shall be rendered on or before the   day following

the end of the quarter for which they are made up and the amount due shall be paid forthwith.

5   The Agents shall not be accountable for bad debts, but shall do their utmost to prevent their occurrence.

6   The Principals reserve to themselves the absolute right to refuse any order, but shall exercise such right of refusal reasonably.

7   The Principals will supply in respect of goods to be delivered to the territory on the day such goods leave the works two copies of all invoices for the agent's own use in addition to the copies required for other purposes.

8   The Principals agree to provide the Agents with all information, catalogues, and samples necessary for carrying on the Agency, such samples to remain the absolute property of the Principals, and to be maintained in good order and condition reasonable wear and tear excepted, and to be returned to the Principals, or otherwise disposed of as they shall in writing direct, provided always that the said samples and catalogues shall be delivered free of all freight, duty, and charges into the port of entry in the before-mentioned territory.

[Alternative for the above clause]

The Principals agree to provide the Agents with all information, catalogues, and samples necessary for carrying on the Agency, such samples to remain the absolute property of the Agents when finished with, the Agents agreeing to bear the cost of freight and duty and incidental charges in connection with such samples.

[Clause occasionally inserted when a large range of samples is carried]

In addition to the above, the Principals agree to pay the Agents a subsidy towards expenses incurred in the above mentioned territory at a rate of £ per annum, payable in equal quarterly instalments.

9   This Agreement shall be construed in all respects in accordance with the Laws of England, and all disputes which may arise under, out of, or in connection with or in relation to this contract shall be

submitted to the arbitration of the London Court of Arbitration under and in accordance with its rules at the date hereof.

IN WITNESS WHEREOF the said parties have hereunto set their hands the day and year first before written.

....

....

Index

217

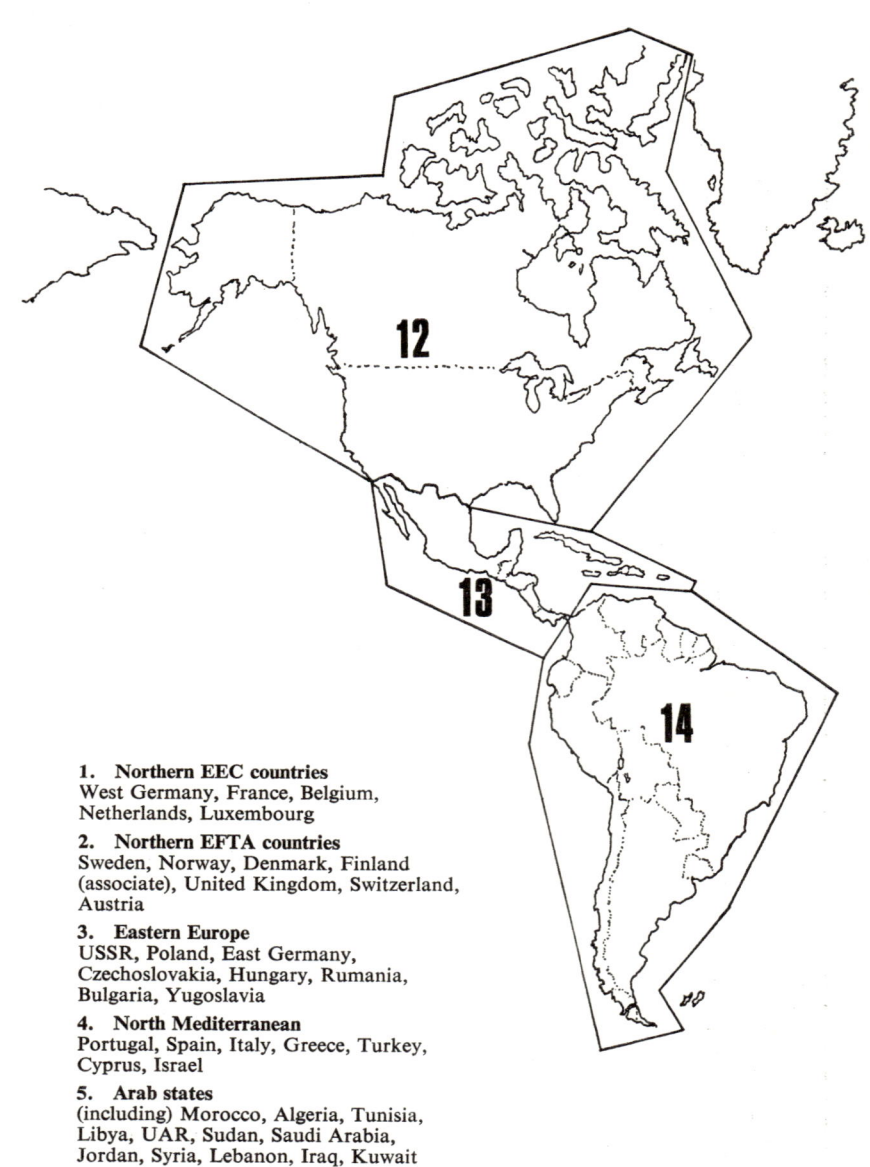

1. **Northern EEC countries**
West Germany, France, Belgium,
Netherlands, Luxembourg

2. **Northern EFTA countries**
Sweden, Norway, Denmark, Finland
(associate), United Kingdom, Switzerland,
Austria

3. **Eastern Europe**
USSR, Poland, East Germany,
Czechoslovakia, Hungary, Rumania,
Bulgaria, Yugoslavia

4. **North Mediterranean**
Portugal, Spain, Italy, Greece, Turkey,
Cyprus, Israel

5. **Arab states**
(including) Morocco, Algeria, Tunisia,
Libya, UAR, Sudan, Saudi Arabia,
Jordan, Syria, Lebanon, Iraq, Kuwait

6. **West Africa**
(including) Nigeria, Ghana, Sierra Leone,
Liberia, Guinea, Senegal, Mali, Gambia,
Ivory Coast, Mauritania, Niger, Chad,
Gabon, Togo, Cameroon, Dahomey